VALUES AND ECONOMIC DEVELOPMENT

The Indian Challenge

VALUES AND ECONOMIC DEVELOPMENT

The Indian Challenge

V. K. R. V. RAO

VIKAS PUBLICATIONS

DELHI * BOMBAY * BANGALORE
KANPUR * LONDON

VIKAS PUBLICATIONS

5 DARYAGANJ, ANSARI ROAD, DELHI-6
SAVOY CHAMBERS, 5 WALLACE STREET, BOMBAY-1
10 FIRST MAIN ROAD, GANDHI NAGAR, BANGALORE-9
80 CANNING ROAD, KANPUR
MOUNT DRIVE, NORTH HARROW, MIDDX, ENGLAND

PRINTED IN INDIA
AT DELHI PRESS, RANI JHANSI ROAD, JHANDEWALA ESTATE,
NEW DELHI, AND PUBLISHED BY SHARDA CHAWLA, VIKAS
PUBLICATIONS, 5 DARYAGANJ, ANSARI ROAD, DELHI-6

PREFACE

Many books have been written on economic development or economic growth and I have no doubt that many more will be written in the coming years. My only excuse for venturing to place this brief volume before the book-weary public is the attempt it makes to view economic development as a problem in values and the role of the human factor in more than the economic sense during the "process of economic development." My attempt has been stimulated by the particular relevance of this view to the problems of democratic socialist development posed before my country and the desperate attempts it is making to initiate and accelerate the process of economic development within the framework of a parliamentary political democracy which is also wedded to the establishment of a socialist order. The conflict and convergence of values involved is the running thread that binds both the sections of this book, the first dealing with the problem in general and the second with the Indian problem in particular.

Almost for the first time in Indian history, the ethical issues in economic development have been squarely placed before the people of my country. Economic growth with social justice has become the accepted creed and the abolition of poverty and unemployment made the central objective of government policy and economic planning. Popular mandate has been sought for a new Indian society, secular, democratic and socialist, to be created by non-violent methods and under due processes of the laws of the land. And the people have given this mandate in categorical and unambiguous terms. The Congress Party has been returned to power at the Centre with a majority of sufficient magnitude to enable it not only to enact any legislation it desires but also to make such changes in the Indian Constitution as it deems necessary for fulfilling its election pledges to the people. The opposition in Parliament has become weak and demoralized, most of its prominent leaders have been defeated at the polls, and what confronts the Treasury Benches in the Lok Sabha is a medley of small and mutually unfriendly groups and not a strong and integrated opposition that can offer the country an alternative government. The ruling party has now no alibi or escape if it fails to fulfil its electoral commitments. The odds are in favour of success if the values are there and are acted upon in practice. If the ruling party fails for one reason or other to satisfy the expectations it has roused in the now politically conscious masses of India, the danger that will emerge is not merely a threat to its own political future; it will, in fact, constitute a threat to the very continuance of parliamentary political democracy in this country.

It is my hope that this book will serve the purpose of drawing the attention of both those who lead and who are led in our democratic set-up to the issues involved and highlight the importance of values and the non-economic role of the human factor for democratic socialist development in my country.

V.K.R.V. Rao

New Delhi
1 May 1971

CONTENTS

SECTION ONE

VALUES AND ECONOMIC DEVELOPMENT— CONFLICT OR CONVERGENCE

SECTION TWO

THE INDIAN CHALLENGE—VALUES AS AID TO DEVELOPMENT

SECTION ONE

Values and Economic Development—Conflict or Convergence

CHAPTER I

FROM A TRADITIONAL TO AN INDUSTRIAL SOCIETY

It is fairly easy to identify a traditional society; but it is not so easy to define it. Tradition means habits, customs, attitudes, and ways of life which get embodied in institutions and then tend to get frozen because of the stability and autonomous existence of these institutions. Thus tradition implies age and, with it, a fairly long period of continuity. It also postulates a certain rigidity that makes adjustment to changing conditions difficult, if not impossible, without the stimulus of some external force. From a philosophical point of view, tradition can also mean values independent of time, in addition to including values that are essentially dated in character. Not all aspects of a traditional society thus need to be changed; at the same time, change is implicit in any traditional society that has continuing life in it. A traditional society can be progressive in some of its content, while a progressive society will always have in it some traditional elements. In terms of social dynamics, a traditional society tends to acquire some of the characteristics of a progressive society as it moves forward in time; while a progressive society tends to acquire a traditional bias as it grows older.

All societies are therefore somewhat mixed in character if

one takes an overall view and not confine one's attention only to the material content of human progress. Hence it is that one cannot talk of a secular tendency towards human progress if one extends one's universe of discourse from material facts to ideas. It is true that over the centuries, the conceptions of human equality and social responsibility seem to be finding progressively more extensive recognition in practice, but it is also a fact that we have outbursts of savagery that set the clock back from time to time, though scientific progress proceeds without interruption. That is perhaps the reason why we have the Hindu theory of *avatars*, the Divine Being appearing in human form from time to time to re-expound the moral law and restore its recognition in human society.[1] History thus seems more to take the form of lopsided development and cycles in ethical behaviour, rather than one long and identifiable line of balanced development in both matter and spirit.

In my opinion, therefore, it is better to drop Rostow's concept of a traditional society as the initial stage in the process of economic growth, carrying the implication that it is therefore of a backward character. An additional argument in favour of this view is the point made by Professor Aaron that Rostow's classification places together in one category all societies which are not developed. I think it would be more correct to talk of progress in productivity, rather than progress as such, when talking of the change from ancient to modern societies. This would be so even when one accepts

---

[1] This is given in the clearest and most authoritative exposition in the *Bhagwad Gita* where Sri Krishna, addressing Arjuna, affirms, "Whenever there is decay of righteousness, O Bharata, and there is exaltation of unrighteousness, then I Myself come forth; for the protection of the good, for the destruction of evildoers, for the sake of firmly establishing righteousness, I am born from age to age."

the concept of development as the creation of a scientific or industrial society as postulated by Aaron, or the growth of rationality as suggested by Ginsberg. This is because science, industry, and rationality, all of which are inter-connected, constitute means rather than ends, which latter is to be found in the ethical and spiritual development of human personality.

I would therefore confine myself in this chapter to the concept of development as material or economic change, and examine the problems that confront a society which is trying to change its economic position in the direction of increased income, larger wealth and more of the material content of human well being. I would prefer to call this process the change or transition from a pre-industrial economy to an industrial economy rather than from a traditional to a modern society.

The main characteristic of a pre-industrial economy is an overall low *per capita* income. In other words, production by the community, or its annual output of goods and services, is not sufficient to give its members a decent minimum of food, clothing and shelter to satisfy basic human needs, even if the output were equally distributed *per capita*. But in fact there is no equal distribution, with the result that the economic condition of the masses is even worse than is justified by low national productivity. A small minority has a much higher standard of life, and uses its command over resources either for more consumption or for putting up buildings or maintaining an army or encouraging art or culture or religion. The result is the paradoxical existence of a society backward in its economy but quite often advanced in art, architecture and aesthetics, or in religion and philosophy, or in military might, or in a combination of them all.

The economy of such a society is usually distinguished by agriculture being its most important activity. Then there are the cottage industries producing low-value goods mainly intended for the limited requirements of the masses, and catering to a large number of small markets and linked with rural self-sufficiency. There are other cottage industries, largely urban-centered and, producing high-value luxury commodities to meet the requirements of the rulers, noblemen, landlords, priests, and other rich sections of the community. The tertiary sector consists of services—domestic, military, and artistic—all intended for the consumption of the rich. Priests, medical men, transport services, commercial services, judicial services, and police services cater for the requirements of the community as a whole, but with their accent on the needs of the richer classes. Priests and teachers usually go together, and secular education only takes the form of apprenticeship training in arts and crafts. The occupational pattern is thus conspicuous for the comparative absence of secular education, science, technology, banking, and corporate enterprise. Methods of production followed are traditional, and largely primitive; there is no application of what is now called science and technology. Implements used are simple and power used is mainly human or animal, with some wind power. The result is that economic activity is predominantly labour-intensive.

The economy described above is accompanied by a society sharply divided into classes. The actual workers, whether on land or in industry or in services may or may not be the decision-makers for their own production. Thus, some may be working for their feudal, priestly, or princely bosses and being looked after in return, while others may be owner-cultivators or independent artisans or priests or warriors or medical men selling their services for remuneration. But common to them all is the low level of their disposable income, and the appropriation of a part of their income or output by some one or other in authority.

Thus workers consumed less than they produced; and insofar as the surplus was not theirs to dispose of, either for consumption or investment, they were an exploited class. The result was that they had no incentive to step up their output by additional inputs or labour; nor were they able, even if willing, to increase their production through invest-ment. The natural result was that workers had no special interest in increasing their efficiency and did not therefore put forth their creative effort for increasing production.

But this is not to affirm that no surplus emerged from agricultural production. Those who appropriated the sur-plus, viz. princes, noblemen, landlords and priests, did use a part of it for providing artificial irrigation by canals and water-works.[2] Marx, who admits that this distinguishes what

---

[2] The role of government in ancient and medieval India in pro-viding public works of this kind is well known. What is perhaps not so well known is the part that temples also played in this field, and the possibility that they perhaps constituted the "voluntary" agencies which were used by the state for the coordination of state funds in irrigation works. Cf. Burton Stein: "That Hindu temples in South India followed the practice of utilizing money endowments to produce new irrigation is not new information. In the present study, based upon the inscriptional record of the Tirupati Temple, it has been possible to examine in much greater detail the way in which this operated. More significantly, however, this detailed study has made it possible to indicate the important role of the state in the temple programs of irrigation and development. The degree to which the Tirupati Temple depended upon state donors in the 16th century (about 90% of the village held by the Temple and about 50% of total monetary endowments) suggests a fruitful area for further re earch. In particular, it raises the question of the extent to which other temples, similarly involved in land development, received the major portion of their resources from state donors, and hence, the proportion of state resources indirectly allocated to temple-sponsored land development. More generally, the participa-tion of the state in irrigation development at Tirupati raises the question of whether the apparently localistic economic organisation

he calls Asiatic society from Western society, erred in attri-
buting it to a lower level of civilization in the Orient and a
greater capacity for forming voluntary associations in European peoples.

It must also be admitted that a part of the surplus went
with the construction of *dharamshalas* (rest houses at pilgrimage centres) and *chatralayas* (hostels) for Vedic
scholars. But this could not be productive investment in
the economic sense, though it had an undoubted role in
the promotion of cultural unity. Forts, churches, mosques,
temples, palaces, and mausoleums constituted the bulk of
the capital created by this society. The natural result was economic stagnation. Those who were interested in production
did not have the surplus and those who got the surplus were
not interested in production. It is true that a part of the
surplus went into the hands of the money-lending and
mercantile classses who came into existence to meet the
consumption requirements of both the masses and the
classes; but they used this surplus primarily to get a larger
share of existing wealth and thereby increase their liquid
assets and financial power, rather than for increasing production and thereby building up their capital assets as also an
increased income.

It is true that this class later on turned out to be the
harbinger of the new era, their general attitude becoming
progressive and favourable to change, when their accumulating surplus began to be used for productive investment.

---

of medieval South India may not have been integrated thro the
redistribution of state resources to centres like the temples, which
were not essentially economic centres but which had important
economic functions." "The Economic Function of the Medieval
South Indian Temple," *Journal of Asian Studies*, February 1960,
p. 176.

This, however, came later, and it came much more easily to the smaller and sea-faring nations whose traders went out into the world for earning their living than for a vast land mass like Russia or China or India.

The economics of the lack of progress over the centuries is quite simple. Because productivity was low, the rate of savings was low. Whatever surplus was generated in the community was largely used either for wasteful consumption on the part of the upper classes, or for conspicuous consumption at times of births, deaths and weddings or for economically unproductive capital expenditure. Education was mainly in the hands of priests and was not oriented towards the creation of a scientific temper. The priesthood, who formed the intellectuals, and set the pace for progress in knowledge, were interested in a study of the inner man and his spiritual progress, leaving material progress to be achieved by propitiation of the gods rather than by a conquest of the environment. The working masses had but little interest in increasing output as they could not be sure of getting their due share in any increase in production they may bring about. The upper classes were absorbed in fighting, chivalry, religion, and art and looked down upon manufacturing, merchandizing and money-making. They were therefore not particularly interested in economic development.

It is not surprising, therefore, that there was economic stagnation, and this continued till a breakthrough in the feudal system came through the rise of towns, the growth of a mercantile class, and the interest of kings in using these two forces to break the power of the land-owning nobility and the mind-owning priesthood.

The surprising thing about the system was not the continuation of economic stagnation over a long period, but the long continuation of social stability. This was primarily due to the social psychology that accompanied the system as well as to the influence of religion and the traditional attitudes towards classes that it gave rise to on the part of the masses. Thus the idealization of poverty, the philosophy of contentment, the feeling that the individual soul was more important than the social order, and the concept of rendering unto Caesar what was due to Caesar—thus implying the acceptance of the *status* quo in the socio-political framework almost as a matter of a divinely-ordained duty—led to a feeling of acceptance on the part of the lower orders, and made for conformity and social stability. Buttressing it from a different side was the prestige and status attaching to membership of the upper class with what almost amounted to divine sanction behind its superior privileges and ways of life. This gave the social order an authority far greater than any that could have been the result of either the threat or even the actual exercise of superior physical force.

This was why perhaps Marx called religion the opiate of the people. But it can be seen that in the light of the then development of the productive forces of science and technology, this opiate was a functional necessity if society was not to lapse into primitive anarchy, or get into some kind of a primitive communism that would have made impossible the kind of magnificent cultural and aesthetic progress that traditional human societies did achieve in spite of general economic backwardness.

The transition from such a society with its inherent and built-in-strength for self-sustaining continuity to such an entirely different order like the modern, industrial, or scientific society that we know, is a mystery that social scientists have not yet been able to diagnose to their satisfaction. It is still a matter needing explanation as to why the industrial society should have erupted in Europe and not in Asia, though in terms of their pre-industrial wealth, status, and prestige, Asia was perhaps better off than Europe. Even Marx was not able to place Asia firmly in his explanation of the historical process towards economic growth, and had to content himself with a description of Asiatic society and not apply to it that rigorous historical and logical analysis that he did to society in the West. Partly, no doubt, it was due to paucity of material and Marx's lack of access even to such material as did exist. Partly, however, it was un-doubtedly due to certain significant difference in the struc-ture of the pre-industrial society in Asia that he could not fit in with his general analysis.

Since this chapter deals with the current problems of transition towards development, and is mainly concerned with India as a major illustration of the process, it may be worthwhile dwelling briefly on the nature of the traditional society in India, its pre-industrial character, its long period of changeless stability, and the reasons why it has lasted so long and started so late in the development process.

Traditional society in India shared many of the character-istics of other advanced traditional societies, especially in respect of its pre-industrial features. In fact, Indian society was more advanced, insofar as some of the handicrafts, which grew on the basis of extensive court patronage and patronage of the temples, reached a high level of technical and aesthe-tic perfection. As pointed out by Dr Ananda Coomara-swamy, Indian craftsmen were well organized in guilds with elaborate rules, regulating entry and ensuring quality, and displaying a remarkable measure of self-regulation and self-government. Places of pilgrimage and capitals of the major kingdoms provided all-India markets for the finer handicrafts and, as pointed out by many a traveller, gave ancient and medieval India a flourishing urban civilization. The surpluses which accrued, however, went into unproductive capital expenditure and did not lead to the emergence or adoption of productivity-raising inventions or standardized output on a large-scale basis. Society was dominated by caste and the privileges and obligations attendant on caste; and scriptural sanction and priestly influence gave stability and continuity to a non-egalitarian and exploitative society, with the masses functioning as hewers of wood and drawers of water and showing a contentment with their economic lot that was truly pathetic. All this was in common with other traditional societies in a similarly advanced stage.

What was, however, most striking about India was its village community. The Indian village was more than a collection of individuals. It was a closely knit and well-integrated society based on caste and division of labour and functioning on the basis of self-regulation and self-government. Self-government did not, of course, mean the modern panchayat with adult franchise and central assistance. Village leadership was based on status, but status carried with it a code of obligation or duty, and village opinion was usually powerful enough to ensure good government. It is doubtful, however, if every village was self-sufficient in the rigid sense of the term.

As pointed out by Professor M.N. Srinivas and A.M. Shah,[3] there were transactions between villages, especially neighbouring ones, and in some areas, villages sent out their commodities to wider markets. Fairs, weekly markets, and peripatetic traders and artisans formed a link between villages and towns, and villages drew on urban areas for certain spe-

[3] Vide their article entitled "The Myth of Self-Sufficiency of the Indian Village," in Economic Weekly, 10 September 1960.

cialized services, especially in construction work. Taxation also provided a link between villages and the outside world, and so did the not infrequent forays which defeated or victorious armies made into the villages draining them of whatever wealth that could be consumed or removed.

With all this, however, the village and the village system continued more or less intact over the centuries. As Marx points out: "These family communities were based on domestic industry, in that peculiar combination of hand-weaving, hand-spinning, and hand-tilling agriculture, which gave them self-supporting power. . . ."[4] He quotes from an old official report of the British House of Commons on Indian affairs to show that, politically viewed, the village was more like a corporation or township with a number of officials each having defined and separate duties. I shall now continue the quotation:

Under this simple form of municipal government, the inhabitants of the country have lived from time immemorial. The boundaries of the villages have been but seldom altered; and though the villages themselves have been sometimes injured, and even desolated by war, famine or disease, the same name, the same limits, the same interests, and even the same families, have continued for ages. The inhabitants gave themselves no trouble about the breaking up and division of kingdoms; while the villages remain entire, they care not to what power it is transferred, or to what sovereign it devolves; its internal economy remains unchanged.

Marx was quite right in pointing out the adverse effects this system had on the mental attitude of the rural popu-

[4] Marx, "The British Rule in India," article dated 10 June 1853.

lation towards progressive ideas like nationalism, social justice, a sense of control over the environment, and the resulting strengthening of the forces of economic stagnation. Thus, a high price had to be paid for the stability and continuity that the village system gave to Indian society. While this meant parochialism and rigidity in the economic and social sphere, the village showed a remarkable capacity for flexibility and adjustment in the religious field. Perhaps this had something to do with the fact that in religion the village was constantly in contact with the outside world and developed an identification or loyalty that extended far beyond the boundaries of the village.[5]

As Professor Raghavan has pointed out,[6] the epics and the *Puranas* were made expressly to broadcast Vedic lore to the people at large, and this was made effective by an unbroken tradition of deliberate provision, by ruler and teacher, for recitation in the Indian languages of the ancient Hindu epics, especially the *Ramayana*. The stories were not only recited; but they were also expounded; and each expositor, in his own way, made additions that supplied illustrations from current life, referred to immediate problems, and altogether brought a note of realism and modernity into what otherwise would have been just traditional knowledge.

Flexibility and freedom from the narrow and restricting walls of parochialism were also shown by the ingenuity with which local gods got absorbed into the Hindu pantheon and reappeared as parts of a larger system that extended over the community as a whole and gave the village a sense of belonging to a larger world at least in the religio-cultural field. Marx's mistake lay in not recognizing this element of flexi-

[5] Srinivas and Shah, n. 3.
[6] Vide "The Social Organization of Tradition" in Redfield, *Peasant Society and Culture*."

bility and adaptability to new ideas that Hindu society possessed, though this was only confined to the religious and cultural spheres and did not extend to the socio-economic network.

Speaking on the opposite side, Professor Norman Brown claims that Indian history, from period to period, has shown Indian society possessed a unique quality of tolerance "a tolerance of the new, the unusual, and the different, a capacity to reshape itself in changing conditions, a quickness of comprehension and a willingness to seek for new solutions to new problems."[7] It is true that India did achieve a unique and diverse multitude of institutions; but this very tolerance was inhibitive of a spirit of revolt and change, and it gave outdated and reactionary social institutions and customs a stability that is now causing difficulties in effecting the transition to a scientific and industrial society.

This changelessness in Indian society extended itself through the period of the industrial revolution and beyond, when Western society was pulsating with new life and achieving remarkable progress in effecting its transition towards an industrial society and breaking the back of the economic problem. Why this should have been so is partly explained by the quality of tolerance that gave unexpected strength to economically outdated but traditionally nurtured institutions and ideas, and partly by the strength of the village system. Partly, however, the explanation is more mundane. At the very time when mankind in the West was setting out on its great new economic adventure, and readjusting, in the process, its traditional institutions and ideas in the socio-economic field, foreign rule came into being in

[7] Paper on "Class and Cultural Traditions in India" in *Traditional India: Structure and Change*, Ed. by Milton Singer, p. 39.

India. The foreigner, who wanted peace and quiet within the country to facilitate his schemes for colonial exploitation, found himself developing a vested interest in the continuation of India's social stability. The powerful influence of the State was therefore thrown on the side of the social *status quo* and the prolongation of the traditional society.

While this was not powerful enough to prevent the break-up of the old economic order including the village system and the urban guilds, it did succeed in preventing Indian society from getting that initiative and impulse for change so necessary for the evolution of a modern scientific and industrial society. Hence the concentration of progressive Indian interest on the political problem of getting the country rid of its foreign rule. Hence also the delay that has ensued in the transformation of the pre-industrial society of India into a modern scientific and industrial society. It is only with the advent of independence and the installation in political power of persons having a profound and personal interest in the country's economic progress, that India has started on the march towards the establishment of a modern or scientific and industrial society.

Before discussing some of the problems involved in this process of transition, it would be useful to set out briefly the major characteristics of what we call the industrial society and the factors necessary for effecting this change.

To begin with, the major characteristic of an industrial society is a significant increase in productivity, a substantial increase in its output of goods and services, and a noticeable rise in the *per capita* income of the people and their levels of living. This is accompanied by a revolutionary change in its pattern of occupation and employment, with a substantial rise in the proportion of its population occupied in industry, a much more substantial fall in the proportion of its population occupied in agriculture, and a significant increase in the proportion of its population working for wages or salaries or other forms of contract incomes. Methods of production change, with science, technology, machinery and power forming crucial additions to the production system and completely transforming the productive process. Goods and services are now produced more for the market than for self-consumption, money replaces barter, and the economy gets market-oriented.

The market gets enlarged from local to regional, national, and international dimensions; and the economy passes from self-sufficiency to inter-dependence. Production becomes cost-conscious and takes the form of purposive and economic activity rather than being just a traditional way of life. Villages get depleted, people begin to live in larger aggregations, towns and cities grow, and urbanization becomes the dominating feature. There is a revolutionary change in the pattern of investment. While unproductive buildings and military installations continue to occupy their historic place in investment, productive capital gets added to the picture and in fact becomes the leading sector. Investment not only takes the form of more of the means of production but, also, of the means of production of the means of production. This includes economic overheads like transport, harbours, power, and municipal services, industrial staples like iron and steel, chemicals, fuels, minerals, cement and other building equipment, heavy engineering equipment and machinery for making machinery, and social overheads like education science, technology and research.

What are the factors necessary for bringing about this transition to an industrial society? An industrial society obviously requires both the accumulation of capital and the utilization of capital. Accumulation means savings and in-vestment; utlization means initiative, enterprise, and the application of science and technology. It also means organi-zation, management, and the application of rationality to economic activity. All these have human implications and involve the human factor in the economy. I shall describe them therefore in terms of the changes in psychology and pattern of behaviour they involve and which constitute the basis of an industrial society.

Savings in a pre-industrial society are just sufficient for stabi-lity and do not result in economic growth. This is partly because the rate of savings itself is low; and partly because those who obtain control over the available surplus largely use it for unproductive purposes—either wasteful consumption or non-economic capital expenditure. An industrial society needs a significant rise in what I may call the effective rate of saving, i.e. the proportion of resources that is used for pro-ductive capital expenditure. This means a two-fold change in human behaviour, one an increase in the volume of sav-ings either by less consumption from a static income or a non-increase in current consumption from an increased in-come, the other in the direction of a more productive use of savings.

This psychological change in the attitude towards savings-utilization is what Prime Minister Nehru had in mind when he referred to hydro-electric works or iron and steel plants or machine-building factories as the new places of pilgrimage, the old objects of pilgrimage being of course the temples, stupas, mosques and churches on which the savings of the community used to be so largely expended in the past. Thus a change is required in the psychology of both the masses and the classes. The masses must be prepared for reduction in consumption or postponment of increase in consumption, while the classes must be prepared not only for reduction in consumption but also for using their savings in a productive manner.

Secondly, there must be a change in the attitude of the community in general, to income and work. The kind of contentment with poverty and misery that distinguished the Indian masses and led to the widespread use of the epithet "the mild Hindu" no doubt contributed to the stability of the non-egalitarian Indian social order; but it did not make for economic growth.

The first step towards economic change is the development of an attitude of dissatisfaction with the economic present. *The poor must first get dissatisfied with their poverty before they or anyone else will take steps to remove it.* People must want more income if they are themselves to take steps to increase their income or co-operate with others who may want to do so. One can always adopt a superior moral attitude and condemn this as moneymindedness; but wanting more income when one is sunk in poverty is a different kettle of fish from wanting more when one is already well-to-do. That is why even Gandhiji had no use for poverty in the Indian masses. His conception of the *daridranarayana* was not intended to glorify poverty, but to rouse the social conscience of the rich towards the paradox of poverty in man, who at the same time was *Narayana* or God himself. His desire was to stimulate the sense of social obligation of the well-to-do towards those who were badly off.

Thus economic growth requires that the poor give up their "pathetic contentment" and develop a positive demand for an increase in their income. But mere increase in the demand for income will not bring about economic growth. It must be accompanied by the conviction that more and better work is necessary in order to get more income. But this will not come about if the masses are swayed by the belief that Nature and the environment rather than their own effort are the determinants of income and as the former are arbitrary, their income will fluctuate for reasons beyond their control.

Thirdly, it is necessary that the people at large develop a rational and scientific outlook towards life and especially towards economic activity if the country is to make an advance in the economic field. As long as people are superstitious, propitiate gods to overcome their economic difficulties instead of themselves doing so, and go in for astrology, charms and the like, it is difficult for them to develop that self-reliance and initiative without which it is not possible to move from a pre-industrial to an industrial society. A rational attitude results in readiness to give up customs or attitudes that are not rational but merely traditional, and this in turn leads to a scientific outlook and willingness to apply science and technology to methods of production. It also removes hostility to change and gives the community a spirit of experimentation and adaptability to new ideas. To quote Professor Aaron, that economy is progressive "which is alive to results, repudiates tradition, and is willing to change its habits so as to produce more in less time and to produce different goods by using new methods."

Fourthly, it is also important that there should be universal literacy. An industrial society needs a more extensive spread of knowledge than can be transmitted by oral communication. Without literacy, it would be difficult for the labour force to acquire industrial skills and the necessary knowledge about machinery, power and industrial processes. It is also important that people should get machine-minded and take delight in using their hands and fingers as also tools and implements. It also means that the inverse relationship between superiority in caste or social status and intensity of work, especially manual work, that exists in a pre-industrial society should now get altered. All this requires that the educational system and the system of social values should get re-oriented towards economic development.

Above all, the growth of an industrial society requires the emergence of a group of individuals, a class, a party or an authority that is industrially minded, and is dominated by the desire to build factories, mechanize processes, employ power, reduce costs, increase output, and maximize profits or surpluses. It should be permitted to follow its desire, and in fact be helped to do so by the rest of the community both institutionally and psychologically. All industrial societies that have emerged so far in different parts of the world testify to the crucial role that this "industrial elite" has played in economic growth, though its composition, training, remuneration and methods of operation have shown marked differences in different countries and different ideological systems. Thus as Professor Aaron points out:

Through the experience of the Soviet countries, it is now known that the development of the forces of production, which Marx regarded as capitalism's historical mission, can be achieved through the efforts of the State or of a party or a class of aristocratic origin, as well as through the work of private enterprise. We know that centralized planning is as favourable to development as is a market economy.

The characteristic of this class is single-minded devotion to what may be called the "god" of production, a readiness to take risks and willingness to apply new methods to production.

The foregoing account of the factors essential for bringing

about the transformation of a pre-industrial society to an industrial society reveals clearly the important role of the human factor in economic growth. Now the human factor is influenced by tradition, environment, education, institutions and values. What an industrial society requires is that all these conditioning factors should get re-oriented in the direction of increased productivity and accelerated economic development.

CHAPTER II

INDIVIDUAL FREEDOM AND ECONOMIC DEVELOPMENT

Whether in a traditional or a developed society, there is no denying the primary role the individual plays in bringing about economic development. His motivation, values, attitudes, and skills, all determine his economic behaviour and contribution to the nation's economic growth. How far does individual freedom come in as a factor in economic development?

Individual freedom is a complex concept and no one has defined meaning for all individuals and for all times. Broadly speaking, the modern concept of individual freedom means freedom for the common man to function with the feeling that he has both choice and either influence or control in the most important and pervasive aspects of his daily life. One pertains to work and its reward, including in its scope freedom of choice in occupation, influencing the condition of his work, protecting his existing standard of living against any involuntary reduction, and obtaining for himself his due share in the increment of output resulting from increased productivity and economic development. The other pertains to the socio-political framework under which he functions and includes the freedom to have a type of government that he can influence, if not also control. These two freedoms require for their exercise such tools as parliamentary democracy, an independent judiciary, the rule of law, adult suffrage, freedom of association, including the right to form unions and resort to strikes, freedom of speech, freedom of press, freedom of movement, and freedom of occupation.

Individual freedom in this sense did not exist during the earlier stages of economic development. When the Industrial Revolution took place in the United Kingdom in the 18th century and was subsequently extended to the rest of the Western world during the first half of the 19th century, the only freedom that the masses enjoyed was freedom from the personal restrictions that accompanied the feudal order, with contract replacing status, hire for wages of one's labour in place of customary service, and freedom of movement and choice in occupation. There was neither political democracy nor legal recognition of trade union activity in the U.K., while in the U.S.A. there was political democracy but no freedom of association for the worker. Nowhere in the then developing Western world were trade union rights recognized nor any organized attempt on the part of workers tolerated for securing increase in wages or betterment in conditions of work.

As regards the individual freedom represented by political democracy, as stated earlier, it did not exist in the U.K. during the 18th century or even during the first half of the 19th century, from the point of view of the masses. Indeed, before the first Reform Bill was passed in 1830, seats in Parliament were practically marketable products and it was not till 1918 that adult franchise was universalized in that country. Long before then, the U.K. had completed the early stages of its economic development and reached the stage of a full-fledged industrial power. It is true that the United

States did have individual political freedom during the earlier stages of its development, but one important feature of its economy had great relevance in regard to its impact on economic development. Its land resources were so large and population so small that any individual could, for the mere asking, obtain 150 acres of land under the Homestead Act. This facilitated movement of population from the east to the west in that enormous country and enabled individuals with guts, capacity, personality and allied qualities to exert themselves and make a very good living. Conversely, it also identified poverty with lethargy or weakness, wealth with self-reliance and capacity for work, and idealized the go-getter and the money-making entrepreneur. Suppression of worker's rights also became easier because the bulk of the industrial working class consisted of non-English speaking immigrants, while political power rested in the hands of the original Anglo-Saxon population and their friends and associates, though this was done within the framework of a political democracy. The balance of economic and class power was such that irrespective of the existence or otherwise of the framework of political democracy, the power of the State was thrown behind the employer and against the working class. It was the combination of these two factors, namely, a working class that was un-free and a political democracy that was either oligarchic or biased in favour of the employer, that led to the holding down of wages and the exploitation of labour.

It is the building up of the economic surplus and its effective utilization that constitutes the core of the early stages of economic development. The two principal claimants on the surplus were the employer and the worker, or profits and wages. The worker was a spender because his level of consumption was very low, while the employer was a saver, not only because his level of living was not so low but even more because he wanted to invest, and took delight and found fulfilment in economic development. There was thus a functional necessity for economic growth in its earlier stages that wages be kept low and profits kept high. And where the peasant was responsible for a substantial share of the national income as in Japan during the early stages of its economic development, he also had to be squeezed. Exploitation in the technical sense was thus the foundation on which capital had to be accumulated for the achievement of the economic take-off in capitalist development.

Though in a different setting, the same reality also prevailed in the communist States. These States did have trade unions even in the early stages of their economic development, but these were mainly used as workers' agencies for increasing productivity and did not have the right to strike or otherwise agitate in an organized or militant fashion against the State, which constituted the sole employer in the country. While it was the capitalist entrepreneur who encroached on the worker's share of the economic surplus and used it for investment, the same role was played by the Communist Party in the Soviet Union. In both cases, capital accumulation was based on exploitation and increase in that element in the national income corresponding to profits in the capitalist countries, and public resources, whether by way of taxes or net receipts of public enterprises, in the communist countries. As pointed out by Arthur Lewis:[1]

In private capitalism these entrepreneurs have made private profits and have reinvested on private account whereas in the USSR the great increase in profits has been concealed as a "turnover tax" which the planners have reinvested on

[1] Arthur Lewis, Theory of Economic Growth, p. 226.

public account. But in either case, the essential feature of the conversion from 5 to 12 per cent of saving is an enormous increase in the share of profits in national income.

Exploitation did not merely include the holding down of wages. As pointed out by Buchanan and Ellis:

> The remarkable changes in industrial production during the nineteenth century and the urbanisation that accompanied them had their sordid side and were often tainted with human suffering and misery. Only after industrialisation had gone on apace for some time did the social conscience of the times belatedly recognise the evils and dangers of industrialism by enacting legislation affecting hours and conditions of work, safety precautions, urban living, etc. Unemployment, old age, sickness and other problems of economic insecurity were of course recognized as a social responsibility only at a very much later date. Perhaps the pace of industrial advance in the first half of the nineteenth century is therefore partly to be explained by the fact that these social costs of the transition to industrialism were not included in the reckoning.[2]

Thus individual freedom for the masses did not exist in terms of either political or trade union rights during the early stages of economic development. For the classes, however, and especially the entrepreneurial element among them, there was individual freedom that not only permitted them to do what they wanted with themselves and their possessions but also enabled them to restrain or restrict the freedom of others who came in the way of their development activity. The manu-

[2] Buchanan and Ellis, Approaches to Economic Development, p. 142.

facturer, the merchant, the producer, the man who really built up the capitalist economic system was a saver and was not a spender and he had something of a sense of mission. He found self-fulfilment in the increase of his business. There was something mystical in the way in which the individual capitalist went about wholeheartedly concentrating his attention, not on increasing his consumption levels, but on building up his business. He had freedom because legislation restricting his freedom, whether in regard to wage or trade union rights or monopolies and trust etc., came only much later.

The corresponding class to enjoy a similar freedom in the communist world was the planner, the party, and the machinery of the State. I would suggest that the party in a communist society took the place occupied by the entrepreneur in the early stages of economic development. Both were inspired by a passion for economic development, with this difference that motivation was personal in the case of the capitalist entrepreneur while it was collective and society-involved in the case of the communist entrepreneurial class.

The important point that emerges is that the industrial revolution preceded the political revolution in the capitalist world; and both the beginning and crucial stages of industrialization coincided with the denial of individual freedom to the masses. Nor does economic development in the communist countries tell a different story insofar as the crucial stages of their industrialization is concerned. Thus, in the capitalist or communist countries, whether in the past or the present, the early stages of economic development appear to be almost inevitably linked with the absence of individual freedom for the masses.

All this should not be taken to mean that individual freedom as defined earlier is a negative factor in economic development. It all depends upon the stage of development and the motivations and attitudes of the people who are participating in the development. Development requires people who will be willing and able to take advantage of the opportunities created by the existence of natural resources and new methods of exploiting them. Individual freedom for the entrepreneur or his counterpart in the communist world has certainly helped in the early stages of development while a similar freedom does not appear to have been necessary in the case of the masses.

This dichotomy between individual freedoms is essentially, therefore, a historical phenomenon associated with the early stages of economic development. It was only as the economy advanced from its earlier to its later and more mature stages of development that the masses were required to play a more volitional and active part in the process. It was only then that power got dispersed, political and social institutions become more democratic in actual content, and individual freedom got broadened to include larger and larger sections of society that belonged to the masses and not only to the classes. The process is still under way in the capitalist countries and has just begun to operate in the communist countries. Thus, historically speaking, individual freedom for the masses appears to be an end-product of economic development rather than an essential condition during its earlier stages.

CHAPTER III

SCIENCE, TECHNOLOGY, AND ECONOMIC DEVELOPMENT

To a layman, the relation between science, technology, and economic development seems obvious and positive. By and large, economic backwardness is the result of lack of understanding of the laws of nature and inability to direct their working to any desired end. Conquest of the environment and using this conquest for a manifold multiplication of the supply of goods and services is the very essence of the economic development which began with the Industrial Revolution of the 18th century and is continued at an accelerated pace by vast funds currently spent in the developed countries on R & D (Research and Development).

Science provides knowledge and technology, the tools for the harnessing of natural resources, the development of machinery to exploit them, the gigantic power needed to drive the machinery, and the skills and know-how required for operating the machinery. The result is a vast increase in the output of known consumption goods and services so that they become adequately available for mass consumption and the creation of new goods and services first on a small and then on a mass scale.

It is not necessary to list the achievements of the last two centuries in terms of either the magnitude or the components of economic growth. Many books have been written on this subject and the conspicuous differences in levels of living between the scientific and industrial societies of the West (which now also includes Japan and Australia in their universe) and the traditional and backward societies of the East—with India figuring prominently—that are now trying desparately to get on to the road towards economic development. What is important to note, however, is the crucial relation that exists between economic development and the development of science and technology. Whether it is in agriculture or in industry, in transport or in communication, in entertainment or in sports, in residential or office accommodation, in medical services or child welfare, the supplementing, if not in many cases the replacing, of man by machine has conspicuously reduced the incidence of human drudgery, and made for a life of greater comfort, variety and increased leisure for vast numbers of people in the developed societies, and a few people in positions of power or affluence in the developing societies. It is obvious therefore, that a major task for the economic planner in the developing countries is the development of science and technology with particular reference to the resources and needs of the country and population he is planning for.

Science does not mean only teaching and research in the physical, biological, chemical, mathematical, or other allied scientific disciplines. It also means the creation of a scientific temper, the belief that every effect has a cause that can be discovered by the application of logic and research, confidence in human ability to overcome the obstacles created by a hostile environment, and increasing disregard for superstition, charms, astrology and all irrational explanations of natural phenomena and the ascribing of unexplained or unexpected events to the play of supernatural process. The creation of such a scientific temper is needed not only among scientists but also among the masses, if traditional and economically backward societies are to move forward with the world of economic development, mass welfare, and reduction in the real cost in time and labour of material production. This is a matter to be taken up not only by those in charge of education but also by those in charge of mass communication media in the developing societies.

Apart from the creation of a scientific temper or climate among the masses, economic development also requires a large task force of scientists, including students, teachers, and researchers. We need both fundamental science and applied science; and while there can be more liberty for fundamental science, there has to be more direction and objective-directed work in the field of applied science. Research effort has to be planned and conducted according to the particular needs of the country concerned with a clear perspective of the psychology and motivation of their scientists, technologists, administrators, and industrialists. In addition to science teaching in colleges, and teaching and research in university departments, special research laboratories should be established in both the public and private sectors. The government of developing economies should have a definite and clearly enunciated scientific policy and a department of science development. At the same time, effective coordination should be established between the relevant government departments, research laboratories, and industrial enterprises in order to get adequate dividends from the nation's investment in scientific research.

When we consider how science can help increase productivity through inventions, innovations and adaptations, technology plays a major role. In early times, industrial art was more a matter of experience and application rather than the result of the impact of scientific research. It was only in the latter part of the 19th century that science began to have a decisive impact on technology and that made countries like Germany, which pioneered in scientific research, to assert their superiority in industrial development. Science indicates the possibility of a thing to happen. It is technology that translates the possibility into practical reality. The research scientists in laboratories can generate new ideas and test the efficiency of a process or a product upto the pilot plant stage. The economic feasibility of the processes, and acceptability and adaptability of the products have to be proved by bringing on the market technically good products. It is for the industrial enterpreneur to take up the responsibility for this task and face the challenges of scientific advancement. They must also be prepared for the risks of failure in translating the results of the research into practical operations in the factory or in the field.

In the innovation chain, research is only a stage. The other and more important stages are pilot plant trials, process development and design of equipment, fabrication and erection of plants, manufacture of products, sales promotion, and so on. Research laboratories are mainly concerned with the first part, the experimental part which is comparatively less expensive. Development of the processes on a pilot scale and design and fabrication of equipment are all expensive, and constitute the responsibility of industry. Unless the effort of industry is closely matched with the effort of our research laboratories, the gap between research and its application to production will continue to widen.

Ours is an age of impressive scientific and technological achievements. Television and radar, electronic computers for the solution of complex mathematical problems and business accounting, semi-conductor devices, electron microscopes capable of magnifying 100,000 times and more, nuclear fusion and fission processes for power generation and for the production of radio-active materials that are of importance in agriculture, medicine and industry, new synthetic materials for a wide range of applications to industry and in our daily life, gas turbines and jet propulsion—these are but a few examples of the tremendous achievements of our modern world. These and others in practically every field are the results of the creative efforts of scientists and technologists working in many countries as partners in a common enterprise to extend the frontiers of scientific knowledge and to apply scientific discoveries to practical technological problems. They emphasize the interdependence among the various branches of technology, as well as the ever increasing dependence of technology on fundamental sciences. They have further demonstrated the increasing need for technologists to acquaint themselves with, and to interpret and apply, the work of chemists, physicists, metallurgists, and mathematicians, as also the need for the representatives of various scientific and technological disciplines to collaborate in their work.

It is therefore axiomatic in economic planning for developing countries that science and technology play a decisive role in increasing agricultural and industrial productivity. The mere availability of science and technology, however, does not automatically ensure economic development. If science and technology are to contribute to productive processes, the country needs quality scientists and technologists who, while possessing specialist expertise, also understand the inter-relationship of different disciplines and are able to coordinate a diversity of skills, techniques, materials, and experience to solve engineering problems. They must be in coherent communication with each other in order to identify the main areas of national importance, in which fundamental research is needed, and indicate how the results of such research can be projected to the industrial plane. In the last analysis, it will be their expertise and know-how, and their ability for coordination and their motivation for using their skills, that will determine whether minerals stay underground   or are transformed into goods useful to man, whether oil remains hidden or becomes a major source of power and heat, and whether roads remain mud-tracks or are transformed into arteries of trade and commerce.

In determining the place of science and technology in economic development, one should be. careful in applying without reservation the concept of self-reliance which is otherwise an accepted objective for economic growth of a self-accelerating character. The concept of self-reliance in scientific research and technological development needs to be considered against the background of the current store of technological knowledge available in the contemporary world and the level and perspective of scientific development in the developing country. It would obviously be unwise to work out, or rediscover on our own, technological know-how available elsewhere and wait till we do so for setting up the relevant industrial units merely to satisfy the otherwise laudable urge for self-reliance. In developing countries, time is the great hurdle and we must do in a few years, what the developed countries have taken a few decades to achieve. Our problem is not only to bridge the technological gap but also halt its widening. Therefore, if technological know-how can be obtained on suitable terms the developing countries should not allow themselves to be deterred from doing so by any considerations of false prestige.

Borrowed technology, however, may need modification or adaptation to suit the requirements and local conditions of the country concerned with special reference to raw materials, markets, and skills. Apart from adaptation, borrowed know-how and knowledge should be used as a basis for further research, experimentation and innovation, so that it becomes possible for the developing country not only to narrow the technological gap but also go ahead of the developed countries in new processes and products. An excellent example of this sensible use of borrowed technology is Japan, which has surpassed the originating countries in many fields such as electronics, ship-building, chemicals, and instrumentation. Economic development thus requires a careful and deliberate effort not only to build an indigenous scientific and technological base but also make use of the available technological know-how in the contemporary world and then strive to surpass it by sustained effort in scientific and technological research in appropriate coordination and collaboration with industry.

The economic motivation underlying the growth of science and technology in the developed countries is the desire for more goods and services for mass consumption. It is this that has made research and development such an important component of economic development and stimulated the flow of such large funds for the purpose in both the public and private sectors. The resulting large-scale effort in mass production, fresh varieties, and new goods has led to certain side effects that were not anticipated by the proponents of a sustained and constantly increasing rate of economic growth. Atmospheric pollution, spoilation of the life-giving elements contained in both fresh water and sea-water resources, disturbance of the historical balance between the various components of life and materials achieved by nature over many tens and hundreds of centuries, rapid exhaustion of natural resources of economic importance, not to mention the growing tensions and psychological disturbances created by industrialization and urbanization, and the failure of faith and values to counter the process—all these are now found sprawling and in an unlovely fashion in the developed world dominated by the ideology of economic growth, unlimited wants, and unhealthy competition for personal aggrandizement. A special effect of this new society on the younger generation is a sense of disillusion with the charms of affluence, a feeling of frustration because of its lack of appeal and challenge to their moral conscience and a spirit of revolt that lacks direction and takes all kinds of forms such as hippism, drug addiction, anarchy, violence, and extremist political activities. It is clear, therefore, that while science and technology is an essential instrument for economic development, it has not been an altogether unmixed blessing even in material terms, apart from its impact on ethical standards and spiritual values.

The adverse material results of the indiscriminate use of science and technology for economic growth has now reached such dimensions that it has attracted governmental and scientific notice both at the national and the international level. Governments of the highly industrialized countries are now appointing Ministers of Environment and Pollution and international organizations are arranging symposia and seminars at the expert level to determine the causes and extent of the damage and possible remedies for the same. Policies are now under formulation both at the national and international level to dilute, if not actually eliminate, the adverse consequences of the application of science and technology for the creation of affluent societies with large-scale production and mass consumption of increasing varieties of goods and services. A great deal of discussion is also under way on the problem of the revolt among the youth, and social scientists are busy trying to formulate policies and programmes that will give the youth a sense of participation and achievement and also instil in them values that will bring about peace and contentment. Developing countries therefore should take warning in time, and while using science and technology for economic growth, take care to see that its adverse effects are minimized if not eliminated by an appropriately formulated pattern of development.

As regards tensions, ethical behaviour and values, it is necessary to discuss separately the relation between ethical and economic development. And this is what we propose to do in the next chapter.

CHAPTER IV

ETHICS AND ECONOMIC DEVELOPMENT

Economic development definitely involves the stimulation of a desire in the individual for a better level of living. If he is content with poverty, then he will neither be interested in the creation of opportunities for economic development nor will he make use of them even if they are otherwise made available. To the extent that the ethical or religious beliefs that prevail in the country either idealize poverty or justify inequality in income and opportunities, the mainspring of economic development would be missing.

Economic development thus requires a materialist code of ethics that sets value by material possessions and makes their attainment a matter of virtue as well as profit. It also requires the giving up of any traditional ethics that includes beliefs, superstitions, and ways of life that come in the way of maximizing production or reducing costs or increasing marketability. Competition, getting ahead of the other fellow, seeing the fulfilment of one's personality in the magnitude of one's material possessions, not allowing sentiment to interfere with one's economic activities that are aimed at profit or maximization of one's income, in short, acceptance and application of the economic calculus for the regulation of one's economic activity is a determinant of the pace and magnitude of economic development.

To the extent that ethical values or religious belief come in the way, they have to get subordinated in the interests of economic development. Insofar as ethics is concerned with unselfishness, compassion, subordination of one's personal interest to something larger than oneself and restraining the desire for maximizing one's own personal welfare, ethical development has to take a subordinate place and adopt a conformist attitude in the interests of economic development.

Thus there is a certain antithesis between ethical and economic development which comes to the surface as soon as a backward economy sets out on the road to economic development. National policies and patterns of behaviour have to be directed towards the subordination of ethical to economic development. The antithesis referred to was most clearly stated nearly 2000 years ago by Jesus Christ when he said: "It is easier for a camel to pass through the eye of a needle than for a rich man to enter the gates of heaven."

It is also relevant to note that the beginnings of the Industrial Revolution and the era of economic development it inaugurated were marked by the emergence of political economy or economics as a separate discipline, with Adam Smith talking of the economic man and outlining the economic calculus needed for maximizing economic activity and its fruits. Only, as Adam Smith was the Professor of Moral Philosophy in Glasgow University, he attempted a reconciliation of the economic with the ethical, by the suggestion that a divine hand saw to it that the pursuit of self-interest by the many led to the maximization of welfare for all the individuals taken together or the community in general. It was this suggestion that gave a philosophic foundation to the policy of *laissez faire* and free enterprise; and gave respectability to the divergence that emerged in practice between ethical values and economic activity.

The early years of economic development accompanying and immediately following the Industrial Revolution were filled with economic activity that involved a gross violation of ethical or human values as has been amply illustrated in the works of J. L. and Barbara Hammonds. Then came a revolt against the doctrine of *lassez faire* and the accompanying glorification of the economic man by the socialists, the co-operators, the religious humanists, the sentimental literateurs, and finally the economists themselves, who talked of welfare as distinguished from wealth, and the divergence between the social product and the private product of economic activity. These had a perceptible effect in softening the rigours of economic development and bringing about political and social changes that were more in tune with ethical values. In other words, the beginnings of economic development and the earlier years of its progress were at the expense of ethical development, while the later years of economic development witnessed a resurgence of ethical development or at least a recognition of ethical values in the ordering of economic activity.

The two centuries of economic development that the world has witnessed since the Industrial Revolution cannot be said, however, to be distinguished by land-marks in ethical development. From time to time, of course, there have been such spurts as the movement associated with Cardinal Newman in the 19th century England or the Oxfam movement during recent years in the same country, or the increase of philanthrophic activities, with a number of wealthy people using a part or whole of their well or ill-gotten wealth for the purpose of education, hospitals, art galleries and museums, and the development of research. The state has also changed its complexion in the developed countries from a police to a welfare state, while communist economic development has also seen the communist states giving special attention to the provision of welfare and cultural services as a part of their governmental activity.

On the other hand, the same period has seen some of the bloodiest wars in human history and abandonment of the laws of chivalry that previously confined the fighting and killing mainly to the classes, leaving the masses largely unaffected by their operations. We have also seen during the same period the horrors of the Spanish Civil War, the genocide and pogroms aimed at Jews and fantastic atrocities and violations of human dignity witnessed under Fascism, Nazism, and the earlier, insecure periods of communism. Scientific and technological development that has brought efficiency to economic activity has rendered the same service to the armaments industry and methods of war, culminating in the dropping of the atom bomb on Nagasaki and Hiroshima and recently in the happenings in Viet Nam. Even the developing countries have shown themselves in tune with this new phase of horror and inhumanism in the Biafra massacres and with the recent military attempts to destroy and denigrate hostile civilian population in East Bengal, which has declared itself as Independent and Sovereign Bangla Desh. On the whole, ethical development does not seem to have accompanied economic development and the new age of science and technology with which it is associated.

More recently, a new danger has arisen to the continuing progress of economic development. And that is the extent to which the indiscriminate and unlimited use of science and technology for the promotion of economic activity based on the concept of unlimited wants and mass production, has led to the emergence of side effects that are beginning to threaten the continued maintenance in the future of economic activity on the scale it has currently assumed in the developed countries.

Long ago, Professor Pigou drew a distinction between the marginal social net product and the marginal private net product and gave striking examples of the way in which the ignoring of this divergence led to a diminution of social welfare. The economics of welfare that he drew attention to, and for which he formulated policies for the regulation of the private economic product in order to reduce the diminution of the social product and bring about its maximization, have become far more relevant today in the context of the affluent societies of the developed world, and their mad race for a higher and higher rate of economic growth in spite of the high levels of living already reached in these countries.

In fact, the subject of man in the biosphere has now become of great importance in the academic world, and some of the best scientific and technological brains in the world today are engaged in finding antidotal or curative measures for dealing with the materially adverse present and future consequences that are resulting from the gigantic and expanding mass production characteristic of the affluent societies.

Apart from this danger to the very foundations of economic development which form its materialist base, modern society is also witnessing the emergence of social, psychological and ethical aberrations resulting from unlimited economic growth and the fall in spiritual values and the resulting frustration and confusion of mind and emotion that accompanies it. Affluence is now presenting its own evil side, even as poverty presented its evil side during the earlier centuries, and ethical development seems to suffer as much from affluence as from poverty though in different ways. What seems clear to me is that the world cannot afford this imbalance between ethical and economic development whether in the traditional or the industrial societies and that what we need is a right balance between ethics and economics, what Vinoba Bhave would call integration of science with spirituality, or what may otherwise be termed as the integration of economic development with spiritual values.

One cannot do this unless one abandons the crude idealization of the economic man and the unbalanced ideology of unlimited wants and the current quest for continually increasing affluence in the developed world. Economic activity is only one part of human activity and it bodes ill for the rest of human activity if the former were allowed to dominate all human activity. Economic activity only constitutes means to an end; and that end is the all round development of human personality rather than the mere multiplication of material goods and materialist services. At the same time, account has also to be taken of the fact that economic activity consumes a large part of the time of the human being and therefore the nature of this activity has a direct impact on the development and fulfilment of human personality.

Thus economic activity should not only be treated as a part of human activity and its growth therefore brought in balance with the non-economic activity, but economic activity itself has to be recognized as constituting both ends and means from the point of view of the development of human personality. That was the reason why I selected for my inaugural lecture of 1942 as Professor of Economics in the University of Delhi, the subject of the nature and purpose of economic activity. I quote below what I summed up in that lecture:

Economic activity is of the nature of both the ends and means activity, and its purpose is to secure exchangeable goods and services possessing economic value but in such manner as (a) to satisfy the fundamental minimum requirements of the community for economic goods, (b) to occasion the maximum use of resources and ensure avoidance of waste in each act of production and (c) not to hamper but foster and promote the end of all human activity, namely, the development of human personality.[1]

To this I would now add not to go in for processes or scales of operation that would adversely affect the continuance of economic welfare in the future. Above all, the need of the hour is the recognition of the principle that economic development is but one aspect of human development, and what we should aim at, is human development as a harmonious whole of which, of course, the economic constitutes an important and possibly crucially important component. Economic development therefore has basically to be in line with ethical development though the emphasis may shift from one to the other depending upon the stage one has reached in the development of the country concerned. The methods adopted for economic development therefore cannot be divorced from ethical values nor indeed the goals of economic development from the values, whether ethical, spiritual or aesthetic, that have always taken the highest priority in human thinking and the development of human personality.

How this integration is to be brought about is still an unsolved problem. What is clear, however, is that means and ends are interdependent variables, private gain is not necessarily consistent with public welfare, material well-being has

---

[1] Vide "Nature and Purpose of Economic Activity," *Essays in Economic Development*, 1964, chp. 1, p. 24.

to be reinforced by moral well-being, and economic activity has to accord active recognition to the non-economic aspects of human life. The ancients extolled poverty and the moderns have gone in for affluence. Both have failed to secure peace and happiness. What is needed is a compromise admixture of the material with the spiritual, want with restraint, and ethics with economics. It is this lesson of economic development that should not be lost sight of by the developing countries which in their desperate quest for material growth are tending to forget the values and the ultimate purpose for which economic development is only a means and not an end.

CHAPTER V

SOCIAL AND ECONOMIC DEVELOPMENT

It should be obvious from the preceding chapter that development is much more than a process of economic growth and increasing national income. In fact, it is part of a process of social change and ethical values that leads to the creation of a whole new society. What we want is an integrated view of human development, where the variables are not only economic but also social, ethical, political, and psychological if not also spiritual and value-oriented, and the end-product arrived at is a better and more fulfilled human being.

Some of the links between social organization, traditions and values and the development of an industrial and scientific society have been already referred to in the first chapter. It is also necessary to comment on the popular belief that social development is something that follows economic development, that attention should therefore be concentrated first on economic growth, and that problems of social growth can be taken up only after problems of economic growth have been successfully tackled. This is based on the idea that social development requires funds and resources, that resources can only be raised by economic growth, and that therefore one must first have economic growth, after which alone one can go in for social development. Thus social development is regarded as an end-product rather than a contributor to economic growth.

It is utterly wrong to draw this kind of distinction between social and economic development in terms of time-phasing. Of course, actual programmes of both economic and social development might have to be phased with due regard to the circumstances of each case. But to give time-priority to economic growth and suggest that there can be no social development without economic development and also, by implication, to deny that any causal relationship exists between social and economic development is a lop-sided way of looking at the problems of development in general. In fact, one has to take an integrated view of development of which economic development is but one part, social development is another part; and there are also many other aspects of development which also form a part of the general phrase "development."

When we talk of economic development, it does not merely mean investment in material terms. In fact, specific and separate mention of investment in material resources and investment in human resources would be a more accurate way of describing the development process. If one talks of investment all the time, and means only material inputs and material investment, then by implication, the value judgement is formed that all outlays on other than material investments are not productive, that they therefore constitute what are called welfare items, and therefore post-ponable items, with the result that whenever there is a cut they are the earliest to get the cut, and the cut which is largest also falls on them.

Now, all these arise only because of our not having clearly understood the fact that social development, to a large extent, is identifiable with investment in human resources.

Once we recognize that social development is not just a matter of philanthropy or charity or display of compassion and so on—not that these are not important—but that it is essentially of the nature of investment in human resources, then we would give them a more important place in all our developmental thinking, and also apply different criteria to social developmental programmes from the criteria we are now applying. The fact that expenditure on things like education, health or social welfare programmes and so on are not treated as investment, not only gives them a lower priority in the thinking of the planners and the others who take decisions on these matters, but also makes for a flabbier performance on the part of those who undertake these activities. The criteria which are applied to judge education, for example, will be quite different if educators themselves were to treat education as investment and not merely as a welfare activity. Similar is the case with the expenditure that is incurred on health programmes, or even on what more strictly can be called the social welfare programmes.

Therefore, from the point of view of enabling social services and social welfare services to get a better hearing and better placing, as also from the point of view of their becoming a more productive investment in human resources, it is important for us to regard them as an investment rather than merely as something that arises because of the general feeling of compassion which is normally associated with these developmental services.

Take a simple example, like programmes for the handicapped. Now helping them, as a matter of charity, to live lives of complete dependence would be one way of social welfare. But helping to train them to earn their own living by giving them the opportunity to make a productive contribution to society, in spite of their handicaps—that is

the difference which will come the moment we apply investment criteria to social welfare programmes, instead of the
more ordinarily accepted criteria of human sympathy, charity, philanthropy, and so on. I saw something of this when
I visited the Orthpaedic Institute in Rouse Avenue in New
Delhi some years back. There I saw a person who had only
stumps for legs and had thought of himself as a beggar dependent on other people, and did not like it, and was feeling
most miserable. But now he had been given rehabilitation
training and equipment in this Institute. He is now able to
earn his own living. The thing that has made him most happy
is the fact that he is earning his own living and is not
dependent, while from the point of view of society, it means
utilization of unutilized capacity. Instead of treating all
these people as only to be helped, we can also make them
work.

Such examples can be multiplied from other institutions
for the handicapped. Blind people, dumb people, deaf people, or otherwise handicapped people, given adequate and
suitable training with, of course, a proper human approach,
get transformed into productive citizens of society. That
is why emphasis should be placed on the investment aspect
of social development, and care taken to see that social
development leads to the promotion of self-reliance and not
to the promotion of dependence. Therefore, the whole
outlook on social development has got to be changed, not
only on the part of the planners not only on the part of
the Government, but also on the part of those individuals
and institutions which are engaged in social welfare work
of one kind or another.

That social services also constitute developmental services,
and that what is called social development is both a part of,
and the cause of economic development and not a mere

follow-up of economic development, does not wholly explain the relation between social and economic development. It is also important to realize that economic development produces social consequences the cost of which is not necessarily borne by those who benefit by economic development. What we need is a social policy formulation which will make a pointed impact on the thinking of the people in regard to the relationship between economic development and social development, and the need for action being taken to deal with the problems of social development that are raised by economic development. The object of the social policy statement should be to see that built into the five year plans are the systems, plans, policies, programmes, institutions, methods and instruments, which will see to it that social development does not go by default in the course of economic development.

As a matter of fact, every student of social and economic history knows that economic development creates many social problems, and dealing with the social problems that are created by economic development should be the major study of social policy. Social policy, therefore, should essentially deal with the social problems that arise as a part of the process of economic growth and constitute also a part of the cost of economic growth. Dealing with these problems, therefore, should also be treated as a part of the investment that should be made in order to see that economic growth does not lead to imbalances in social growth, and all Plan programmes should be judged from the point of view of how far the economic development it creates also provides the preventive, protective, curative, institutional and reformative services for the social problems that arise as a result of economic development.

It is not necessary to go into the details of these social

problems. We all know what social problems arise when there is urbanization, or migration, or land reform, or a selective approach in promoting agricultural production, or even when there is extension of education, or of health activities. But we do not always pay attention to them. Sometimes we do not even recognize them, whereas proper planning demands that we anticipate them, identify them, and take remedial measures in time.

Take family planning programme for example, and the social problems that it will lead to in a society which hitherto had, on the whole, fairly good norms of sexual behaviour. We must recognize that a reduction in the birth rate brought about by deliberate and extensive governmental programmes of family planning also leads to other consequences. Reduction in the birth rate is not going to come about by Gandhian self-restraint. This is going to come about by the adoption of technical methods which are going to remove the normal connection between sex relations and procreation. When there is talk of sterilizing millions of males and females, or distributing hundreds of thousands of intra-uterine devices or of making contraceptives like condoms available *ad lib* like chocolate and cigarettes, as in drug stores in the United States, then it is also necessary to anticipate the effect all this is likely to have on sexual morality and take the necessary social steps by way of education and rigid controls on pornographic literature, posters, films, etc. that have the effect of stimulating the sexual appetite. Take a simple thing like cinema posters. Having lived in Delhi for the last 30 years, I have seen things which appear on the cinema posters today which never appeared thirty years ago.

This is only to illustrate the general thesis of the need to anticipate social consequences of economic programmes and take action to neutralize the effects that may adversely affect social development. It does not mean that we can give up family planning. For example, if we have nuclear energy development, it may also facilitate the production of the atom bomb. But this does not mean that we should give up development of nuclear energy. The relevant point is the importance of anticipating the social consequences and the social problems that arise from economic growth and then taking steps to see that these are countered simultaneously with the growth of the economy. Take even education. When a rural boy gets educated, he thinks his father is a fool, he develops contempt for his ancestral occupation, and does not want to reside in the village. Education is a good thing, we cannot stop education because of that, but we have got to see that something is done by which this kind of result does not take place.

So almost anything that is connected with economic growth that is desirable and must be undertaken, also throws in its train social problems, problems of relations between men and women, parents and children, sisters and sisters, brothers and brothers, citizens and government, class and class, communal groups, neighbourhood groups, and so on. It is the duty of the planner to anticipate these side effects of economic development and devise measures for dealing with them.

What is not yet understood in many developing countries is that economic development throws in its train a series of social problems which, if they are not met and countered and properly dealt with, in time may lead to a position where though we may garner a large number of fruits, they may turn out to be bitter and biting in their taste. It is important therefore to undertake research on this subject and study the consequences of economic growth in terms of their effect on social relations, social institutions and social attitudes. If the effect is good, it must be promoted. If it is bad, then it must be countered by appropriate measures of an antidotal or protective or curative or reformative character. What is needed is an integrated programme of social policy for dealing with the problems that arise in the social sphere as a result of economic development.

CHAPTER VI

CAPITALIST AND COMMUNIST DEVELOPMENT

We have reviewed in the previous chapter, the problems that arise in the course of development from a traditional to an industrial society and the relation between economic development and individual freedom, science and technology, ethical values, and social development. The running thread that connects the five chapters in this section is the need to view development as a whole process, of which economic development is but a part, the need for balanced growth of these components for the promotion of harmonious development, and, above all, the overriding role of human factors with special reference to the psychological and value considerations involved.

In this chapter, an attempt is made to review the relevance of the politico-social framework under which the development takes place by taking two systems that are popularly supposed to be directly opposed to each other, namely, the capitalist and communist systems, and examine the similarities and differences revealed in their methods of economic development, again with special reference to the human factor and the psychological and value aspects involved.

Economic development involves such utilization of a country's national and human resources as will give its

people the maximum possible income per head, along with
the capacity to maintain this income and ensure a reasonable
rate of annual increase. This means not only economic growth
from a given base to a pre-determined target, but also the
inclusion in the economy of a built-in rate of further growth.
It is recognized that the initial upward movement in income
may involve the use of foreign aid; but foreign aid cannot be
an indefinitely continuing feature of a country which has
undergone economic development and obtains the status of
a developed country. A further condition of economic
development therefore, is, that within a reasonably short
period, the maintenance of the higher level of income reached
as a result of development, as also the securing of a built-in
rate of continuous growth, does not require foreign aid. That
is why economic development is identified not only with a
significant rise in the national income per head but also with
the establishment of what is termed a self-reliant, self-sustaining, and self-accelerating economy.

Economic development as described above requires for
its implementation, certain essential conditions which are
independent of capitalist or communist ideology. These are
briefly: (1) Increasing the current rate of investment and
along with it the current rate of saving. (2) Directing and
operating the increment in investment in such a manner as
to increase the output of consumer goods, of producers goods
and of productive skills. (3) Saving and investing a substantial portion of the increment in income resulting from the
increase in investment. (4) Directing and operating the
additional investment to increase the output of producer
goods, consumer goods, and skills.

The operational part of development is the increasing of
investment, the pattern given to the increased investment,
the efficiency with which the additional investment yields

an increased output of goods and services, the extent to which the increased income is saved and invested, the pattern given to the additional investment, and so on till the circle is completed and starts again.

Coming to the more difficult part of the subject, namely, the difference between the capitalist and the communist methods of economic development, there is no standard definition of capitalist economic development, nor is there a standard definition of communist economic development. Thus, for example, the economic development of Great Britain has not followed the same pattern as that of the United States, and neither of them have followed the same pattern as that of Japan, and yet they are all capitalist economies. Similarly, there are significant differences in the pattern of development followed by the Soviet Union, Yugoslavia, Poland, and China, and yet they all count as communist economies. All the same, it is possible to indicate broadly the features which characterize capitalist development as distinguished from communist development.

Capitalist economies leave to the individual entrepreneur the major role in economic development. The decisions which are taken regarding consumption and saving, the volume and pattern of investment, and the product-mix are all decisions taken by individuals. These decisions are taken in response to the stimuli offered by the market, which again is a compound of decisions regarding purchase and sales taken by individuals. Means of production are owned by individuals (or groups of individuals combined in partnership or joint stock companies) and it is this ownership with which is linked the power to take the major economic decisions, viz. what to produce, how to produce, and how much to produce. The individual recipient of income, whether from labour or property or from both, decides what to buy, how much to buy, and how much to save. The decisions regarding production are linked up with the ownership of property. The decisions regarding consumption are linked up with the ownership of income, which may be due either to labour or to property, or to both, but in either case it is the individual who is the dominating figure.

The individuals who own property or hire property are the persons who employ labour and it is they who take the economic decisions and determine the disposal of the economic surplus. Prices are given by the market and are determined by the forces of supply and demand, which, in turn, are determined by the pattern of income distribution, the schedule of wants, the state of knowledge and technology, and the dynamism and decision-making of entrepreneurs. Maximization of the difference between price and cost of production acts as the motive force, and profit becomes the determinant of allocation of resources. Private property in the means of production, freedom of individual enterprise, consumer sovereignty, and free play of market forces are the characteristics of a capitalist society, and the entrepreneur is the key figure who operates the system. This is a brief, but not incorrect, description of the capitalist economic system.

The communist system, on the other hand, gives to the community (operating through some person or groups of persons who function on behalf of the community), the authority to take the major economic decisions. There is no private property in the means of production nor is there wage labour hired by private individuals for purposes of production. The means of production are owned by the community; and it is the community which owns and determines the disposal of the economic surplus. The division of income between consumption and surplus is determined by the community. The decisions regarding the volume of investment, the pattern of investment, and the product-mix are all determined by the community. The free market does not exist and prices are more the result of deliberate decision by the community rather than that of the spontaneous play of the forces of demand and supply.

Similarly, the pattern of income distribution is more the result of deliberate decision by the community rather than that of market forces and property relations. Like the capitalist society, the communist society also has prices, incomes, wages and markets, but the forces that determine them are different in the two societies. Thus, in the communist society, the means of production are owned by the community, the community takes on the entrepreneurial function, consumer sovereignty is diluted by the economic decision-making of the community, and the market becomes an instrument for the implementation of this decision rather than a determinant of the volume and composition of the national product. This is a summary of the communist economic system.

There are thus vast differences in the institutional framework and the social philosophy governing the working of the capitalist and communist systems of society. What difference does this make to the methods they follow in the process of economic development?

We have already seen that economic development as such, has certain features that are independent of the system under which it takes place. Accumulation of capital and human skills are both common to the capitalist and communist methods of economic development. The pain involved in the task of accumulation is common to both: and this is amply borne out by the history of development under both the systems. Under the capitalist system, the worker is denied that increment in consumption that he desires and

the surplus gets channelled into investment via the entrepreneur who himself restrains his own consumption (at least
in the earlier stages of development). Under the communist
system the same thing happens, except that the surplus gets
channelled into investment via the state. It would not be
incorrect to describe this technically, as a process of exploitation in the sense of denial to the worker of the whole
product of his labour.

It is this which leads to the emergence of what Marx
called "Surplus Value." What happens is accumulation,
whether capitalist or otherwise. Under both capitalist and
communist systems, such an exploitation of the worker becomes possible because of the absence of political and industrial democracy in the initial stages of development.[1] It is
only as development gets under way and the economy attains
the required rate of saving and investment that freedom, in
the current Western sense, gets established in the institutional framework of the developed and developing society.
Non-voluntary, or at best, involuntary participation by the
working class in the process of capital accumulation is thus
common to the earlier stages of development in both the
capitalist and communist economies. In both, we find the
same accumulation, the same exploitation, the same restraints
on consumption, the same increases of that element in
national income which corresponds to profit in the
case of the capitalist countries, and to public revenues
whether by way of tax surplus or net receipts of

---

[1] For a more elaborate account of this process, and its similarity
under the capitalist and communist systems, see the author's article
on "Freedom and Development—The Challenge with Special Reference to India," *Journal of the Australian Institute of International
Affairs*, August 1960.

public enterprise in the case of the communist countries. Where peasants formed a major section of the community and agriculture contributed a major portion of the national income, as it normally did in the earlier stages of development, the process of capital accumulation also involved the exploitation of the agricultural classes.

It was thus exploitation of labour, both industrial and agricultural, together with the application of new methods of production that enabled the required expansion of the economic surplus and, with it, the capital accumulation necessary for the take-off from pre-development to development. We may not all concede this basic similarity in the real costs of development in both the capitalist and communist societies, but that is partly the result of the normal human tendency to overlook and slur over things that happened in the distant past while simultaneously being shocked and appalled by the identical phenomena if it happens within one's living experience.

This does not mean, however, that there is no difference between the two systems from the point of view of the methods of economic development. In fact, they have followed somewhat different techniques in the process of development; and it is this difference that is of absorbing interest to those of us who come from countries that have either just undertaken or are still to undertake the task of economic development.

To begin with, a communist society must have economic planning, and whether centralized or decentralized, it must be planning on a national scale and, in fundamentals, at the national level. This is the reason why so many people identify planning in common parlance with communism. There can be no doubt that one cannot have communism without planning. But this does not mean that one cannot have planning without communism. Even in a capitalist society, there is some economic planning in the sense of projections, targets, and economic decisions taken in advance of events. Thus, farmers have their plans, industrialists have their plans, the big corporations have their plans. There is a great deal of perspective planning even in a capitalist society. Only these plans are individual or sectional. The decisions that emerge in a capitalist society are the result of the interplay of the decisions taken by a larger number of individuals and of groups, even though these may be based on their own individual plans. Thus, there is somebody taking the crucial decisions in a capitalist society. This is the vital difference between a capitalist and a communist society, not the absence of any kind of planning, but the absence of national planning in the former and its inevitable presence in the latter.

Moreover, the very fact that vital economic decisions are taken as a result of national planning, gives them a greater measure of certainty in implementation than when they are the result of the interaction of a series of individual and group decisions even if these are based on some kind of economic planning. In a capitalist society, one individual's decisions to save may be nullified by another's decision to dissave, whereas in a communist society this does not happen, as the decision to save is taken by the community and not left to the individual. Similarly, one individual's decision to step up investment in basic goods may be negatived by another individual outbidding him in the purchase of factors of production, for increasing consumption. There is no certainty in a capitalist society that anticipated savings will equal actual investment nor is it likely that demands will equal supplies at expected prices. In a communist society, on the other hand, there is a certain measure of certainty in

the savings-consumption ratio, the pattern of investment, and
the product-mix, provided of course the planning is effective
and not just a facade of wishful thinking. Thus national
planning and a certain measure of certainty in the collective
implementation of desired economic decisions pertinent to
economic growth, distinguish the technique of economic
development in a communist society from that in a capitalist
society.

The second major difference between a capitalist and a
communist society—and in some ways following as a consequence of the first distinction—is the higher rate of capital
accumulation in a communist society. This is due to two
factors, namely, a higher rate of saving, and a pattern of
investment more oriented towards accelerating capital accumulation. These two factors act and react on each other
and result in turn in giving a communist society a higher
and quicker rate of capital accumulation.

Let us take the rate of saving first. It is known that the
source of saving in any society, whether capitalist or communist, is the economic surplus. It is the magnitude and
disposal of the economic surplus that determines the rate of
saving in any society. In a capitalist society, the magnitude of
this surplus depends upon the rate of profits, the level of
wages, and the property relations that determine the distribution of the proceeds of production.

Historically speaking, these factors work in favour of a high
rate of savings in the earlier stages of capitalist development,
and it is this factor which led Marx to attribute a progressive
bias to early capitalism in the task of capital accumulation.
But it must not be forgotten that earlier capitalist development coincided in point of time with an unfree society, when
the worker and peasant possessed neither political power nor
class organization and it was therefore possible for exploitation

to increase the surplus. It is also a fact that, during this early phase of capitalist development, the capitalist was a man with a mission who used himself almost as harshly as his workers and restrained his consumption in order to increase the economic surplus. Self-exploitation by the capitalist combined with exploitation of workers and peasants with the help of a State which the masses did not control, and a production mechanism based on property relationships, helped the early capitalist society to achieve a high rate of saving.[2]

What is true of early capitalist development in the 19th century is, however, not true of early capitalist development in the later half of the 20th century; and it is this latter period which is relevant for the discussion of methods of economic development to the underdeveloped countries of emerging Asia and Africa today. In the modern age, where the capitalist system has reached maturity in many parts of the world, with consequential changes in the behaviour pattern of the capitalist, the balance of political power, and the structure of property relations, early capitalist development in the underdeveloped countries suffers from handicaps in increasing the economic surplus which its counterpart did not suffer from during the 19th century when capitalism itself was a new force on the social and political horizon.

A capitalist society in a contemporary under-developed country cannot exert the same pressure on worker and peasant incomes which it could in the underdeveloped countries in the 19th century; and the rate of exploitation, on which depends the size of the economic surplus, cannot be equal to what it was then. Moreover, the capitalist in the con-

2 *Ibid.*

temporary underdeveloped world is of a different brand from his earlier counterpart in the 19th century. He is no longer the man of austerity who treats himself harshly and restrains his consumption in order to increase the economic surplus. When he comes from abroad in the form of private foreign capital from developed capitalist societies, he brings along with him the standard of life and the consumption pattern that certainly does not err on the side of austerity. And when he is a native and claims indigenous roots, he is subject to the demonstration effect exerted by his compeers abroad and foreign capitalists at home, and is therefore not interested in restraining his own consumption and playing that role in increasnig the economic surplus that his counterparts did in capitalist societies in the 19th century. The result is that the capitalist system does not lead to a high rate of saving in the contemporary world of underdeveloped countries.

In a communist society, on the other hand, there is no private ownership of the economic surplus, and therefore, no scope for its utilization for the purpose of increasing consumption. Nor are peasant and worker organizations permitted to play that kind of role vis-a-vis their levels of earnings and consumption standards, that they do in contemporary capitalist societies, whether in developed or underdeveloped countries. In a communist society, there is no capitalist, no owner of private property, no owner of private enterprise, no interest, rent or profit accruing to private individuals, and therefore the whole of the surplus becomes available for savings and investment. There is also no inroad on this surplus by pressure, either political or organizational, of the workers and peasants.

Politically, the workers and peasants are led by the communist party, which has the same sense of mission and plays the same role in regard to capital accumulation as the capitalist entrepreneurs did during the early phases of capitalist development in the now developed capitalist societies. Organizationally the workers and peasants are led by the same communist party, whose emphasis all the time is on production and accumulation rather than on consumption and immediate inroads into the increased production for purposes of increasing consumption. The rate of saving in a communist society is therefore likely to be much higher than in a capitalist society in the contemporary underdeveloped world. Whether it is higher than that in the earlier capitalist phase of the contemporary developed capitalist countries is a subject on which not enough data is available for an objective assessment. In any case, it is irrelevant as far as the contemporary underdeveloped world is concerned, for their interest lies in the rate of saving and how it is likely to behave under the capitalist and communist methods now rather than in the past.

The second major factor responsible for a higher rate of capital accumulation in a communist society is the pattern of investment. The reference here is not to the somewhat futile controversy that takes place in the contemporary underdeveloped countries about the public versus private sector. A good deal of investment that is taking place in the case of a country like India, for example, is no more than the building up of economic and social overheads, the infrastructure, without which economic development is not possible, whether on capitalist, communist, socialist or other lines. In both capitalist and communist societies, as well as other societies which operate what is called a mixed economy, government plays the crucial role in the building of the infra-structure which makes expansion of production profitable for private enterprise and possible for public enterprise.

One should not therefore mix up governmental investment in infra-structure with the pattern of investment that is peculiar to a communist society as distinguished from a capitalist society. When the pattern of investment in a communist society is regarded as more oriented towards capital accumulation, the reference is to investment as between production of consumption goods and production of producer goods, the latter in turn being classified as producer goods for consumption industries, and producer goods for producer industries.

The theoretical basis for this can be traced to Marx and his famous classification of the departments of production, but its importance in contemporary thinking on the promotion of economic growth owes much more to the Soviet experience and their pattern of investment in the planned economic development of their country. In a communist society, the pattern of investment is deliberately planned by central decision, and its emphasis is on the development of producer goods rather than on that consumption goods; and in producer goods, on producer goods for making producer goods rather than on producer goods for making consumption goods. In operational terms, this means a higher priority in terms of time to producer goods for producing producer goods, over producer goods for producing consumption goods, and to producer goods for producing consumer goods over consumption goods. The emphasis is thus more on productivity than on production, more on growth than on current consumption, and more on the future than on the immediate present. The task accepted by the communist system is a high rate of economic growth and therefore the pattern of investment takes the form of a high proportion of capital goods or of capital accumulation in depth, which has a built-in factor for the automatic increase of capital accumulation. Thus, an up-to-date authority on Soviet economic planning has stated recently:

> As the principal branch in the sphere of material produc-
> tion, industry plays a leading and transforming part in
> building up the material and technical basis of socialism
> and communism. The leading branch of industry, heavy
> industry, comprises the foundation of the socialist
> economy, the technical basis for the continuous and
> intensive growth of the productive forces.

This was the reason why the first Soviet Five Year Plan not
only provided for an unprecedented rate of investment
(between a quarter and a third of the national income) but
also assigned to heavy industry about three quarters of the
amount invested in industry as a whole.[3] Moreover, in
actual operation, the rate of investment in heavy industry
was considerably increased over the original estimates, mainly
at the expense of light industry. The growth rate of capital
goods in industrial output was permitted to decline over
the subsequent five year plans, as can be seen from the
table on p. 69 but nevertheless it continued to have priority
over consumption goods and still continues to be the sheet-
anchor of Soviet planning.

---

[3] Yevenko, *Planning in the USSR*, p. 126. Also compare the
latest resolution on the subject passed at the 21st (Extraordinary)
Congress of the Communist Party of the Soviet Union held in
Moscow in 1959. "The Communist Party of the Soviet Union
attaches paramount importance to the development of industry,
particularly heavy industry, which is the foundation of socialist economy and of the might of the country. Moreover, it is the decisive
factor in the development of the productive forces and in the growth
of labour productivity in all branches of the national economy."

AVERAGE ANNUAL GROWTH RATE OF GROSS INDUSTRIAL
OUTPUT IN THE SOVIET UNION

| Period | Percentage for industry as a whole | Of which | |
		Output of the means of production (Group A)	Output of articles of consumption (Group B)
First Five Year Plan (last quarter of 1928-1932)	19.2	28.5	11.7
Second Five Year Plan (1933-1937)	17.1	19.0	14.8
Three pre-war years of the Third Five Year Plan (1938-1940)	13.2	15.3	10.1
Fourth Five Year Plan (1946-1950)	13.6	12.8	15.7
Fifth Five Year Plan 1951-1955)	13.2	13.8	12.0
Seven Year Plan (1959-1965)	8.6	9.3	7.3

In the case of a capitalist society, on the other hand, the emphasis is more on consumption goods, and producer goods for producing consumption goods than on producer goods for producing producer goods. The pattern of investment is, in historical terms, more on capital accumulation in volume rather than in depth, more on horizontal than on vertical expansion. While reducing the strain caused by capital accumulation, it inevitably prolongs the process and makes for a lower rate of capital accumulation and, to that extent, therefore leads to a lower rate of economic growth. It is not possible to be dogmatic about the system of priorities followed in the pattern of investment in capitalist develop ment, partly because we do not have enough data on the subject and partly because of difficulties of interpretation arising from the very nature of investment in a capitalist society which is the result of the interplay of many and uncoordinated individual decisions. But it would not be incorrect to say that, by and large, the priorities in capitalist development have been more on consumption goods and producer goods that would lead to an immediate increase in consumption goods, than on producer goods as such. This has been well illustrated by Hoffman's study of the growth of Industrial Economies, where he has shown that the proportion of consumption goods in their industrial output was very high during the earlier stages of industrial development in a number of capitalist societies and gradually declined with the growing maturity of these economies. He sums up in the following table the overall trend he found in industrial development by analyzing the changes in the relationship between the net output of consumer goods and capital goods industries in a number of economically developed countries.[4]

In fact, the proportion of consumer goods in industrial output has declined to about 30 per cent in recent years in the major economically developed countries such as the

NET OUTPUT OF CONSUMER AND CAPITAL GOODS INDUSTRIES AS A PERCENTAGE OF TOTAL NET INDUSTRIAL OUTPUT

| | Stage of Industrialization | | |
	First	Second	Third
Consumer-goods industries	83%	71%	50%
Capital-goods industries	18%	29%	50%

[4] W. G. Hoffman, *The Growth of Industrial Economies*, p. 97.

United States, the United Kingdom, Germany, Belgium, and Japan. Thus, there is no difference between the capitalist and the communist systems in regard to the place occupied by capital goods industries in the economy; only, the process has taken a much longer period of time in the capitalist countries, as earlier priorities were on consumption goods. In the case of the communist countries, the time taken has been shorter, as earlier priorities were given to capital goods and that too by deliberate and centralized decision.

The combined effect of extracting a larger investible surplus and following a pattern of investment that places more emphasis on producer goods industries, has thus led to a higher rate of capital accumulation in the Soviet Union. This, in turn, has led to a higher annual rate of economic growth in the Soviet Union than in the capitalist economies. This is well illustrated in the following table:

ANNUAL RATES OF GROWTH IN INDUSTRIAL OUTPUT
1860-1958 PER CENT (COMPOUNDED)

Period	UK	USA	Germany	France	Italy	Sweden	Japan	USSR
1860 to 1880	2.4	4.3	2.7	2.4	—	—	—	—
1880 to 1900	1.7	4.5	5.3	2.4	4.5	8.1	—	6.4
1900 to 1913	2.2	5.2	4.4	3.7	5.6	3.5	3.8	4.8
1913 to 1925-1929	0.3	3.7	0.3	1.4	2.6	1.6	7 5	1.1
1925-1929 to 1938	3.1	—0.9	3.5	—0.7	1.7	5.4	6.5	17.2
1938 to 1958	2.9	5.3	3.5	3.6	4.3	3.5	3.4	8.9

So far we have been dealing with differences between the capitalist and communist methods of economic development that have rebounded to the advantage of the former. We may now turn to some other differences which work in the opposite direction and perhaps show the capitalist methods of economic development to better advantage.

A major difference between the capitalist and communist systems is the performance of agriculture in the national economy. The technical methods followed for the development of agricultural productivity and expansion of agricultural production have been the same in both communist and capitalist economies, namely, mechanization and modernization, increase in size of operational units, use of tractors and other farm machinery, and increasing inputs of chemical fertilizers, pesticides, etc.

But communist agriculture has not shown the same results in terms of productivity and output as communist manufacturing industries. Nor has it given the same results as agriculture in the capitalist economies. The numerous crises through which Soviet agriculture has passed beginning with the great Kulak-liquidation and collectivization started by Stalin, the changing role of the machine tractor stations, the continuing (and in a way, gradually extending) existence of a private sector and a free market within the collective farms, the association between the rise of Khruschev and his image as the one person taking agriculture the most seriously among Soviet leaders and determined to solve its problem, the recent decree on an increase in the prices of Soviet farm products with its attempt to improve the terms of trade between Soviet agriculture and Soviet industry and between the rural and the urban sector—all these furnish ample evidence of the uneasy bed that the communist system has provided to agriculture in the Soviet Union.

The comparative failure of the communist system to solve the problem of agriculture has been demonstrated even more clearly by the changes that have taken place in Yugoslav and Polish agriculture with their virtual repudiation of the basic Stalinist concept of Soviet agriculture. And the most recent addition to the testimony has come from communist China which has now admitted the existence of a formidable agricultural problem, following the initial slogan of the "Great Leap Forward" and the universal establishment of agricultural communes, and has therefore officialy proclaimed a policy of slowing down of the great leap forward in its agriculture. Thus, the peasant-led communism of China seems to have shared with the worker-led communism of the Soviet Union the same experience of stresses, strains and disappointments when it came to dealing with agricultural production on the basis of communist ideology.

All this has been in contrast with the experience of agriculture in the capitalist societies led by the United States, where the problem has been one of how to deal with increasing agricultural productivity and rising agricultural surpluses. This comparative failure of communist agriculture both as compared to communist industry and capitalist agriculture cannot be explained away in terms of differences in scientific knowledge and technical skills. It is fairly clear that the explanation is to be found basically in the differences between the two systems in terms of (i) ideology or psychological outlook, (ii) agrarian structure, and (iii) investment policy and priorities.

One gets the impression that communist ideology does not show any special favour to the peasant community. It is true that the party is called a Workers' and Peasants' Party, but the industrial worker, the urban resident, occupies the pride of place. By and large, communist theories, practices and slogans are linked with the worker who is identified with the proletariat, but workers meant, in practice, primarily industrial workers rather than even the poor peasants. The latter were regarded as socially less advanced, and ideologically not fit to assume leadership because of their continuing subjection to feudal ideas and complexes. In fact, one of the acknowledged tasks of the communist society was to bring about a transformation of the peasantry and make them approximate to the industrial working class in their psychology, discipline and capacity for coordinated and collective action. Thus, in some sense, the peasant in the communist society—and this has been so even in China, in spite of the peasant-base of its communist party and the declared peasant-bias of its leadership in apparent contrast to that of the Soviet Union—felt himself a second class citizen rather than one of the elect. This must have had some connection with the comparative failure of agriculture in communist societies to keep pace with their industry in productive efficiency.

More important than this psychological impact of communist ideology was that caused by the changes in agrarian structure which communism brought in its train. Communist theory repudiates private property in the means of production and this applied to land as well. Private peasant agriculture therefore was brought to an end, the Kulaks (or the more well-to-do and efficient farmers who generally also employed hired labour to assist them in farm operations) were liquidated, and collective farms became the ruling form of the communist agrarian structure.

There were two major difficulties that appeared in their operation and were, in fact, inherent in the new structure. One was the difficulty of linking the distribution of farm output sufficiently with individual contribution to production on the farm, with a consequential reduction in the individual incentive for maximization of output. The other was the undeniably adverse affect that absence of private property in land had on the former's incentive for maximizing his effort. This was practically the universal experience of collectivized agriculture, in both the older and the newer communist societies, and led to the abrogation of collective farming and the virtual restoration of private property in land in two at least of the communist countries, namely, Poland and Yugoslavia.

Even when it continued—as in the case of the Soviet Union and some of the other East European communist societies and now in communist China, the system was diluted by the introduction of a certain element of private agriculture in the collective farms and the opportunity given for the sale of its output on a legally recognized free market.

In spite of that, difficulties continued to exist in the task of maximizing farm output and, as has been already mentioned, communist agriculture failed to keep pace in efficiency either with that of communist industry in its own society or of capitalist agriculture as in the U.S.A. or even peasant agriculture as in Japan. Human psychology seems to be such that private property in land used for agriculture makes for a far more positive role in the stimulation of productive capacity than appears to be the case with machinery and manufacturing industries. This contention is supported not only by the experience of industry in the Soviet Union and other communist countries but even by the experience of capitalist economies in the field of industry. Thus, in capitalist economies, private property is far more actively associated with enterprise and decision-making in agriculture than in the case of industry, where share holders in giant corporations like Imperial Chemicals or Imperial Tobacco or Unilevers, for example, play hardly any role in decision-making.

The third factor making for a lower record of efficiency of agriculture in the communist system is the smaller volume of investment directed to agriculture, and the lower priority it is given in the overall pattern of communist investment. The reason for this differentiation between agriculture and industry in the communist pattern of investment, is, in all probability, directly linked with the communist ideological bias in favour of industry. The conclusion seems to follow that the comparatively lower efficiency of agriculture in communist economies is integrally connected with the nature of communist ideology and is therefore a noticeable disadvantage of the communist as compared to the capitalist system.

The second major difference between the communist and capitalist method of economic development that shows the former at a disadvantage, stems from its centralization of decision-making in economic affairs and the consequent growth of a vast and powerful bureaucracy. While such centralization is of undoubted help in the allocation of resources between investment and consumption, the pattern of investment, and the composition of the product-mix, there is also no denying the adverse effect it has on local initiative, utilization of individual enterprise and capacity for risk-taking, and maximization of individual economic effort in terms both of intensity and of quality.

Under the capitalist system, with its competition, profit-making, and possibilities of unlimited individual reward, individuals wth resources are stimulated to put in their best efforts in their own interest. Adam Smith's "Divine hand" performs the task of reconciling the results of such individual enterprise with collective requirements. Administrative decrees and bureaucratic guidance, even if backed by a strongly organized party and ideological enthusiasm, are no substitute for the direct involvement of the individual in his economic activity through his self-interest and his desire for recognition and emulation.

The result of this bureaucratization of economic organization and centralization of economic decisions is not only a reduction in individual efficiency, but also in the emergence of numerous imbalances in detail. It also leads to an attempt at implementation of decrees through evasion of regulations by different units at the expense of one another rather than by an increase in total resources by invention and improvization. Communist administrators and party officials have been conscious of the built-in dangers of bureaucracy that centralized planning involves, and no item has figured more in communist discussions and internal propaganda than the dangers of bureaucracy. In fact, over the years, communist economic administration has been evolving a system of norms of performance, incentives, piece-wages, socialist emulation, decentralization, and other measures aimed precisely at the defect pointed out, and providing communist substitutes for the competition and the free market of the capitalist system of private enterprise in its effect on the release and maximum deployment of individuals with resources.

The cardinal principle of economic stimulation is inducement. One can take a horse to a water trough but one can't force it to drink. What is true of the horse is even more true of man, especially when the activity desired is not just consumption, but active production. However, communistically inclined a person may be, there is a limit beyond which he will not just do what he is told, even if it is by communist authority. Force, even when backed by idealism, fails beyond a point. Human beings have their own ways of resisting force under any system when it is used to evoke positive responses and these are an essential condition for economic growth. The carrot is stronger than the whip in a developing economy. And this is proved by the fact that the outstanding trend in communist economic administration over the years has been the substitution of the whip by the carrot.

This is illustrated by the system of wage payment given to salesmen in shops in the communist countries. There was a standard wage linked with a minimum quota and extra payments linked with performance in excess of the minimum quota. For practically every economic activity, an attempt has been made to create a norm. Output or performance that reaches the norm gets the normal wage. Exceeding the norm results in extra payment and thus an incentive is provided for increasing the intensity and quality of output of effort by labour. It is also widely believed that the norm is usually kept a little low, so that almost every one gets a little extra payment for exceeding it and also gets the feeling that he is participating in the development of the economy. With all these changes, however, though they are tending to minimize the adverse effect on individual initiative and effort that accompany nationalization of economic decisions, it still remains true that the capitalist system has an edge over the communist system in the matter of work-motivation and individual's response. To that extent the latter is at a disadvantage in terms of overall economic efficiency.

One more difference between the capitalist and communist methods of economic development needs mentioning, that also relates to motivation. A capitalist society is an open society in the sense that no restrictions are placed on the free entry of visitors, import of private capital is allowed, and citizens are free to travel abroad; whereas the communist society is a closed society and is guarded by what has come to be known as the "iron curtain." Apart from the political aspects of the iron curtain or its relation to civil liberties, the "iron curtain" has certain important economic implications of considerable relevance to a developing economy. Economic development under the communist system aims at a rate of saving and investment that is not only high but also higher than what the people would go in for if they had a free choice. It becomes easier to do this if the people are not physically aware of the various consumption goods that people in the developed capitalist countries are having.

After all, basic consumption goods, essential for existence, form a comparatively small proportion of family budgets in western countries. Much of the consumption is of a non-basic character, and it is this which accounts for a lower rate of saving in the developed capitalist countries as also the higher preference for investment in consumption goods. If therefore non-basic consumption goods are kept out of the people's sight, it becomes easier to raise the rate of saving without causing stresses and strains among the people and thus possibly obviating the use of government force for dealing with the same. This is how the "iron curtain" facilitated a larger mobilization of domestic resources in communist countries for purposes of planned investment.

In the case of the non-communist developing economies, the "iron curtain" does not exist, and the field is therefore left free for the demonstration effect of a higher level and larger variety of consumption goods that people in capitalist countries enjoy. Private foreign capital that comes in brings with it foreign capitalists and technicians with levels of consumption that have a big demonstration effect on the local elite and leaders. This effect is further reinforced by the experience of those citizens who go abroad and bring back with them a taste for non-basic consumption goods that they have seen during their foreign sojourn.

The result is that the upper classes in the non-communist

developing economies seek a higher level of consumption and therefore save less; and this, in turn, has a demonstration effect on the common masses in their countries and makes it more difficult to get them to accept austerity during the period of development. To this extent, the "iron curtain" which is so closely identified, especially in its earlier stages, with a communist economy, helps it in having a higher rate of saving than those in the open societies characteristic of capitalist economies.

These are some of the major differences between the capitalist and communist methods of economic development. They do not include political or social differences, such as democracy, civil liberties, class differentiations, inequalities, and other factors that distinguish the two systems from one another. Not that they are not important; only this chapter is concerned solely with the economic aspects of their difference and is therefore strictly neutral regarding the political front.

To sum up, the answer regarding the advantages and disadvantages of the two systems is necessarily of the nature of a generalization and is therefore subject to all the qualifications that any generalization on the comparative merits and demerits of two societies are subject to. Thus, for bringing about capital accumulation, for efficiency in generating, mobilizing, and accumulating the economic surplus, the communist system is more efficient than the capitalist system. Or to put it in a different way, the capitalist system will take a much longer time to reach a given level of capital accumulation than what the communist system is able to do. To quote Joan Robinson:

Compared to a purely feudal system capitalism was a great invention for promoting accumulation. It shifted the balance of power from property to enterprise and got going the process of accumulation. Compared to capitalism, socialism makes the transfer in a still more thorough-going way. Property ceases to exist, and the animal spirits of enterprise drive the whole economy to undertake unprecedented feats. Thus, so far as undeveloped economies are concerned, it seems that socialism is going to beat capitalism at its own game, and the reason that it will do so is that it is a far more powerful instrument for extracting the investible surplus from an economy.

It is not necessary to go into the politics of this conclusion. If one wanted to do so, a gruesome picture can be given of what happened in England in its early industrial history and the place of child labour and so on, all of which makes really horrifying reading. Since it happened more than a hundred years ago no one remembers it now. What happened a hundred years ago is history. What happens today is contemporary politics. And there is a great deal of difference between history and politics.

So far as extracting the investible surplus is concerned, it does appear that the communist system is more efficient than the capitalist system. And, insofar as the size of the investible surplus is an important determinant of the rate of economic growth, the communist system is superior to the capitalist system in bringing about economic growth. In regard to the pattern of investment, the balance of advantages is also on the side of the communist system, because the investment policy of the communist society is, as stated earlier, more geared to economic growth than that followed in capitalist society.

It must not be forgotten, however, that it is not merely the size of the investible surplus or the manner in which it is actually invested that determines economic growth. It is also the efficiency of the operation, the productivity of labour in industry, in agriculture, in transport, and in other sectors of the economy. Regarding the productivity of labour in general, the honours seem to rest more with the capitalist system than with the communist systems. This is because, in the case of the capitalist system, the individual is the basis and motivation is directed towards the individual, while in the case of the communist system, the individual is not the basis and motivation is directed towards the community functioning through its individuals in a mystic way under the leadership of the Party. After all, productivity is not merely the result of having good technical skills, or of having modern machinery, or of having a favourable environment in terms of natural resources. Productivity is also the result of that little something which is the interest of the man concerned in bringing about the maximum production, his freedom to experiment, his freedom to make losses, his urge to express himself, his personality, his dynamism, his drive, his go-gettingness, his "animal spirits" to use Joan Robinson's phrase, in terms of economic activity.

There seems to be little doubt that, in the case of the capitalist system, the individual gets motivated to a much larger extent than he does in the communist system. And that is one major reason why, though the rate of growth is higher in terms of investment goods in the communist system, productivity therein per units of labour in agriculture and in industry even today cannot compare with that in the advanced and developed capitalist societies.

It should be clear by now that neither the capitalist nor the communist systems can claim to have all the advantages. Both have their good points, and both have their weakness. If one were to treat the two systems as students who have appeared at an examination, then an impartial examiner's verdict would be that they have both passed, though it would be also true to say that neither of them can be awarded first class marks. Neither of them is likely to replace the other and they have to reconcile themselves to each other's existence on a continuing basis. That is why the cold war appears so futile to a non-aligned observer who does not owe allegiance to either of these systems. Co-existence of the capitalist and communist systems thus gets its logical basis not only on the balance of military power and international alliances but also on the failure of either to hold the unique key to economic development. That is why one can find an admittedly socialist but also internationally recognized economist like Joan Robinson taking up an apparently ambivalent position in regard to the rival claims of the capitalist and communist methods of economic development. I quote:

> First I argued that the socialist system is well suited to the need of developing economies. Now I am maintaining that capitalism, if it is managed with intelligence and good will, may continue to flourish in economies that are already developed. If my argument is correct, we have to look forward to a long period of co-existence of different economic systems.

One may even go further than Mrs. Robinson and question the very validity of continuing to maintain that there is an irreconcilable distinction between the capitalist and communist systems of economic development. Communist methods of economic development during its earlier stages has a great deal of resemblance to some of the basic features of the early stages of capitalist economic development. And communist economic development in its later stages, as in the case of the Soviet Union in the post-Stalinist era, is increasingly incorporating features that have formed an essential part of the capitalist methods of economic development. The capitalist system in the developed countries is going in for planning, diminished competition, concentration of decision-making on vital economic issues in fewer and fewer hands, and on increasingly diminishing play of volition and individual choice in determining the rate of saving and the pattern of investment.

The communist system in the developed and even developing countries is, on the other hand, increasingly going in for decentralization, motivation directed towards individuals, competition rephrased as emulation, less un-free markets, and increasing use of incentives, inducements and stimulation rather than force, ideology, and administrative decrees. The capitalist and the communist systems are drawing closer and are not showing any inhibition in taking from each other what they will serve them better in the strategy of economic development and the promotion of economic growth: only they are not getting merged with each other. The lines are still separate but they are no longer at right angles to each other. It is true they are moving as parallel lines and are getting nearer each other and hence co-existence will get easier as time passes. From a strictly economic point of view therefore, there is something more academic than practical in setting the one system against the other or in viewing them as two water-tight alternative means to economic development.

It is not possible to conclude this chapter without some reference to the non-economic aspects of this question. Capitalist and communist methods of economic development are both historical facts, and they have both passed the historical test in the achievement of economic development. But, as stated earlier, neither of them has passed with first class honours. There can be other ways of economic development that can take the good points of both and yet avoid the bad points of each. Such a system may be called a "mixed economy" or "a socialist pattern of society" or *Sarvodaya* or Arab socialism or African socialism or Indian socialism. It is not the names that are important. It is the integration of economic development with human and social values, the creation of a social and political democracy side by side with economic growth and development, the reconciling of human dignity and civil liberty with economic efficiency and the conquest of the material world. It is what Acharya Vinoba Bhave calls the combining of science with spirituality, that the developing economies of emergent African and awakened Asia should seek. That freedom and development can co-exist and combine even during the earlier stages of economic development may sound somewhat idealistic. If that is so, I must confess myself an unashamed idealist. I would rather trudge along this path and even take the risk of failing to scale the heights of the highest materialistic mountain rather than ensure success by following methods of economic development, whether capitalist or communist, that have in them elements that offend my sense of human dignity, human equality, human liberty, and human spirituality.

When we in the developing countries of Asia and Africa seek economic growth, let us not be overawed by the authority-claiming voice of the expert economist and his protege, the economic man. Instead, I would remember the wise words with which my favourite economist for this chapter, Joan Robinson, concluded her now famous lecture on "Marx, Marshall and Keynes" which she delivered at Delhi in 1955:

The purpose of studying economics is not to acquire a set of readymade answers to economic questions, but to learn how to avoid being deceived by economists.

So do not expect the economist to guide us in our choice of the method of economic development. By all means, we must listen to him, use his analysis, but we must fill up the gaps he so obviously leaves, ignore the irrelevancies he so unconsciously introduces, and make up our own minds as human beings in search of both material well-being and spiritual fulfilment.

The Indian Challenge—Values as Aid to Development

CHAPTER VII

THE INDIAN PROBLEM OF ECONOMIC DEVELOPMENT

Indian economic development is not based on either the capitalist or the communist patterns. While the economic problems it faces are similar to these two systems in the earlier stages of their development, the methods followed are necessarily different and the problems involved more difficult, because of the fact that India is embarking on her development within the framework of a parliamentary democracy, largely based on the British pattern. The process of development gets further complicated by the federal element brought in by the size of the country and the distribution of governmental power between the Centre and the many States that constitute the Indian Union. The numerous difficulties that this leads to in the process of development and the ways in which they could be met, constitute the subject-matter of the rest of this volume.

Parliamentary democracy is the British contribution to political organization. Under this system, Government is formed by the leader of the majority party or combination of parties in Parliament, members of which are elected by secret ballot on adult franchise. To prevent the emergence of a dictatorship based on a parliamentary majority, and ensure the continuance of people's control over the government, the tenure of Parliament is limited to five years (or more or less, depending on the Constitution) after which there has to be a general election, which gives the people the power to throw out the government or any Minister or Member of Parliament, with whom they are dissatisfied and elect new ones of their fresh choice in their place.

The parliamentary system of democracy also requires for its maintenance the rule of law, an independent judiciary, civil liberties including the right to freedom of speech, association, and worship, a free press and a regulated and visibly impartial system of recruitment to the public services. In many parliamentary democracies, there is a further safeguard for the preservation of democracy through a written constitution that guarantees fundamental rights of citizens, and limits Parliament's power to abridge or eliminate them by providing for a judicial review. Usually there is or should be a prescribed procedure for altering the constitution, for no written constitution can be valid in its entirety for all time, in view of the inevitable change that time brings about in social conditions and values.

This brief summary of the main content of political democracy, taken together with what has been stated in the previous section, should indicate the constraints which a system of parliamentary democracy is likely to place on the process and progress of economic development. In fact, economic development, under both capitalist and communist systems, escaped these constraints because neither of them had a system of parliamentary democracy in the terms described above when they embarked on the process of economic development. The position however is entirely different for a country like India which adopted at the very outset, the system of parliamentary democracy and drew up a written constitution which embodied this system together with fundamental rights, a Supreme Court with the power to interpret the Constitution, a free society, and all the corollaries that accompany this concept. India's attempt at planned economic development has been undertaken under a system of parliamentary democracy and it is its psychological implications that constitute the primary challenge of development for India.

When our leaders fought for Indian freedom and succeeded in making us a sovereign nation, we all thought that our troubles were at an end, that a new millenium was in the offing, and that we could now lean back and enjoy the fruits of victory What we forgot was that Independence was only the beginning of a much longer and harder struggle that we had to wage against poverty. The battle against mass poverty calls for a much more collective effort, greater discipline and more sustained heroism than the battle for Independence. Independence only gives us an opportunity for entering on this battle under our own leadership and with a better chance of success. By itself it does not give us victory. It is this hard implication of freedom that I am afraid we have not fully realized.

Freedom of course is a must for any self-respecting nation. We are proud of our new nation state and shall defend it even with our lives. But the very maintenance of national freedom requires economic strength, a basic content of freedom itself being economic development and the securing of a decent standard of life for our people. This cardinal fact was, in truth, recognized by our great leader, Jawaharlal Nehru. That was why he set up the Planning Commission and himself took over its Chairmanship. That is also the reason why the Five Year Plans have dominated our economic life during the last so many years and that is why we still swear by planning as the key to our economic development and the attainment of mass welfare.

There is no doubt that our Five Year Plans and the economic effort initiated and stimulated thereby have yielded results. In spite of the set-back that the Indian economy has received during recent years and the mood of pessimism and listlessness generally prevalent in the country, there is no doubt about the reality of the economic growth that has taken place in India since the inception of planning. There is no need to support this thesis with statistics of national income, agricultural production, industrial output, and the like. One can see for oneself the reality of the economic change that has taken place if conditions, for example, in the partitioned Indian Punjab of 1947 are compared with those that prevail in the Indian Punjab of today.

And yet there is also no denying the fact that public discontent and public dissatisfaction are much greater today than when our *per capita* income was much lower, when our industrialization had not yet assumed a massive shape, and our agricultural productivity was notorious for being one of the lowest in the world. Employment and educational opportunities are much greater in number and superior in reward than was the case before we started the planning era in the Indian economy. And yet we are more angry, more dissatisfied, and more critical than we were when we were worse off. It is time that we examined this paradoxical situation with all earnestness and got back for planning, economic development, and the battle against poverty, the same faith, the same tenacity, and the same enthusiasm that we so readily display when we are challenged to fight for the defence of our national frontiers.

I think that part of the explanation is the very fact of development. When one is impossibly poor and sees no hope of escaping from that condition, one develops an attitude of fatalistic pessimism and lapses into what a distinguished statesman once described the Indian scene as, "pathetic contentment." But as soon as one starts climbing from abyssmal poverty, one wants to climb higher and faster. When the masses begin to feel that poverty is removable and mass welfare attainable, then they undergo a revolution of rising expectations. Political freedom, democracy, self-government, elections, economic development, all these whet the appetite for growth and betterment, and give more vocal and strident articulation to that appetite. It is no good telling a man who is now getting one and a half meals a day that he should feel better because he was only getting one meal a day in the past. What he now wants is two good meals a day, if not three, and he does not care one bit about what he was getting in the past. He is much less willing to tolerate the state of affairs today, when a few much better off, even if that few is increasing in number, than when he thought that foreign rule and the fruits of previous births were responsible for economic inequality. The new graduate who does not get employment is not particularly enthused by the fact that many more graduates now get employment than when his father or his father's friend or acquaintance became a graduate. He is more bothered by his own chances of getting employment and sees with dismay the growing number of registrations in the employment exchanges. The very fact of independence, self-government, democracy, and economic development has made the poor more impatient with poverty and more intolerant with inequality. It is not paradoxical that discontent grows with development. What should surprise us is that the discontent is still held in leash and that the masses have not broken out in revolt in response to their discontent.

The fact of the matter is that while there has been economic development in India, the rate of economic growth has not been adequate. A major portion of the growth in national income has been absorbed by the growth of population with the result that per capita income has grown at a much slower rate. Moreover, because of the accent on capital formation in the national product natural to the early year of development and the gestation period involved in its translation into an expansionary effect on consumption goods, the full results of development have not been felt in terms of the standard of living. Foreign aggression in 1962 and 1965 and the consequent increase in defence expenditure have reduced the resources available for productive investment and thus led to a slackening in the growth of output, while increasing unemployment and the recent sharp inflationary rise in prices have added to economic discontent and pessimism.

The failure of exports to rise adequately to meet the demand for imports has aggravated our balance of payments problem, while massive injections of foreign aid, though affording a temporary solution, have now reached a level at which they constitute a further aggravation of the balance of payments problem on account of the amounts involved in payment of interest and repayment of capital.

Apart from difficulties of external finance, the lack of availability of internal resources or rupee finance is also leading to a slackening of investment in both the public and private sectors with the result that there has been no appreciable acceleration of investment for some time now. Another disquieting factor is the fact that even when we get a bumper harvest and a substantial addition to rural income, we are not able to step up our investment because of the difficulty of tapping a part of this additional income for resource mobilization.

In fact, resource mobilization is our biggest headache today, both in rupee terms for domestic expenditure and in terms of foreign exchange for external expenditure. Deficit financing is no answer to a shortfall in rupee resources nor is foreign aid a satisfactory answer for financing developmental imports. The only adequate answer is a substantial increase in the domestic rate of saving and a substantial increase in the rate of growth of exports. In a way, both these factors merge into one in the sense that what we want is a massive effort on the part of the community to refrain from consuming a significant portion of the incremental output resulting from development, and make it available for domestic outlay on the one hand, and exports and foreign exchange outlay on the other, both for the purpose of financing accelerated domestic investment.

To do this is not going to be easy, especially in the context of India's urgent need for more consumption and the voting power acquired by the masses in our parliamentary democracy. And yet, we cannot afford to give up our desire for a high rate of economic growth if we want to fulfil the pledge we gave ourselves when we attained independence and then spelt out this pledge in some detail in the directives of state policy that we wrote into our Constitution. Nor can we forget that we have gone on repeating and reaffirming this pledge in successive elections both in election manifestos and meetings and in ministerial pronouncements and parliamentary declarations. We have to do in the economic field in two or three decades what took several more decades in the countries that started earlier in the race for economic development, and this we have to do under a system of parliamentary democracy.

To do this, we want a massive increase in the rate of saving. Our current rate of saving is round about 10 per cent. This has to be doubled and we have to aim at a domestic rate of saving of at least 20 per cent of the national income for a period of not less than 20 years. This does not mean that we reduce current national consumption by 10 per cent. What it does mean however is that the incremental income accruing from development should be diverted towards savings to a much larger extent than we do with our current income. In economic terms, it means a marginal rate of saving of 30 to 40 per cent for the next few years, over and above maintaining the current rate of saving at its existing level of 10 per cent of the total national income.

It is obvious that such a massive marginal rate of saving will affect not only the rich, the near-rich, and the middle classes in the country but also the lower middle class as well as the many poor who constitute the bulk of the country. The entire country has to share in the saving effort, the rich as well as the poor, the capitalist as well as the worker, the landlord as well as the peasant, the university professor as well as the primary teacher. Both urban and rural India have to contribute their due share to the national savings.

It is not impossible to do so. Other countries have done it for their economic development, both capitalist countries and communist countries. In both cases, it has meant a postponement of present enjoyment in the interests of future fulfilment, and a tightening of a certainly expandable belt for the masses, under capitalist leadership in the one case, and proletarian leadership in the other. In both, there has been compulsion and exploitation, whether voluntary or involuntary being a matter of opinion.

In our case too, we cannot escape this primal law of economic development, which is the accumulation of savings and its accelerated expansion by turning the savings into suitable investment and following up with the appropriate utilization of the proceeds of such investment. Only our

task is more difficult, as we have to get everything done by
consent and under the constraints of a live and working
democracy. We cannot succeed unless we create in the
masses the psychological preparedness to give up something
in the present for getting something more in the future.
This means that the masses should be willing to save a part
of the increment in their current income that accrues from
development. But the masses have a current income which
is not sufficient to give them even the bare means of subsistence, let alone anything like good food or clothing or
shelter or education or health services. They see with their
own eyes and in their vicinity, whether in the large cities
and small towns or in the large villages and the small ham-
lets, fellow-citizens whose incomes are much higher than
theirs and who not only can afford good food, clothing, housing, education, and, health services but also parade their
ability to do so by their style of living and conspicuous consumption.

Yet, on the political plane, they are all perfectly equal, because India is a political democracy, with one man having
one vote, whether he is prince or pauper, landlord or la-
bourer, employer or worker. Against this imbalance in political and economic equality the masses have been constantly wooed by the candidates for Parliament, irrespective of
their party affiliations, with promises of a better deal and
more of the material things of life if they or their parties
were returned to Parliament. Economic democracy, social
justice, a socialistic pattern of society, and democratic socialism are all phrases and concepts that have been shower-
ed on them in abundance during the five general elections
that the country has witnessed since Independence. And
these have certainly had their inevitable psychological effect
on their thinking and added fuel to the fire of their rising

expectations to which reference has been made earlier as the first fruit of our emergence into independence.

It is not, therefore, going to be easy to get the masses to tighten their belts or forbear from asking for an immediate betterment in their current intolerably low levels of living, nor is any professional politician who knows on which side his bread is buttered, going to run the risk of losing his election or his ministerial office, if he has one, by telling the masses that they must not consume the greater part of the increment to their wages or income when the increment referred to is itself small and the income to which the increment is to be added is not sufficient even for a subsistence level of living.

The sacrifice that this means is genuine as far as the masses are concerned and constitutes what the economist would call "real costs," whereas in the case of classes whose current incomes certainly given them a minimum acceptable standard of living, the sacrifice involved is not of the same intense quality. If those who sacrifice by saving a part of their incremental income suffer a greater hardship, they will not psychologically be prepared to do so unless they feel that there is equality of sacrifice on the part of those who are better off than themselves. Equality of sacrifice does not mean arithmetical equality of all personal incomes. That would neither be practical nor indeed would it be desirable if we want to maximize personal contributions to domestic output. But equality of sacrifice would mean that people whose incomes are at a reasonable level of comfort should not seek to effect any further rise in their immediate standard of living by the increments that may take place in their incomes because of the opportunities offered by economic development.

In effect, this means a temporary ceiling on large incomes

and a near 100 per cent marginal rate of saving in the case of those whose incomes exceed this ceiling. I know that this will not be liked by entrepreneurs, managers, engineers, technicians, bankers, doctors, professors, civil servants, etc., all of whom have a crucial role to play in the process of economic growth and are at present motivated to do so largely by monetary incentives. But if we want a massive rise in the rate of saving and investment, and without it there can be no accelerated economic development — and if we want to bring about rapid economic growth within the context of parliamentary democracy and the political power it gives to the masses from whom resources have to be mobilized, and with their consent, in order to reach the desired rate of saving, then there is no escaping the logic of the contention for a near 100 per cent marginal savings rate for those with large incomes. If the classes will insist on monetary incentives that will give them high personal incomes and a standard of living largely at variance with those of the bulk of the people, the masses are also bound to resist any inroads on the increments to their meagre current incomes and they can enforce this resistance as long as we function as a democracy. Under these circumstances, monetary incentives that we offer for the classes will work as disincentives for savings and even hard work on the part of the masses, and economic development will prove inadequate to meet the challenge posed by the revolution of rising expectations.

What is being suggested may sound an essay in foolish idealism; but there are occasions in history when idealism is the most realistic of all the alternative solutions to a challenging situation. It should be added however, that in order to implement what has been suggested, economic motivation of a personal character has to get, if not replaced, at least adequately diluted by an accepted ideology. Democratic socialism is the only ideology that can secure the conscious and disciplined participation of the masses in achieving the breakthrough to a self-accelerating and self-sustaining stage of economic development. Democratic socialism does not mean a hand-out to the poor or a mere redistribution of current incomes. It means hard work, consistent discipline, and austere living on the part of the masses. Their dividends will come in the form of significant economic, social and cultural betterment but only in the future.

For the present, the developmental process can only offer them a meagre rise in their living standards and accompany it with a demand for harder work and larger savings and expect them actually to work up enthusiasm in satisfying this demand. The classes too, in turn, would need the strength of an accepted ideology for inducing them to put in their best without the incentive of larger monetary rewards. And the ideology for them cannot just be democratic socialism as in the case of the masses, but also the maintenance of the democratic system and the fulfilment of the obligations imposed on their superior talents and position by Indian traditional values. Sacrifice and not acquisitiveness, service and not selfishness, giving rather than receiving—all these have to become a dominant part of the psychology of all who belong to the middle and the upper classes. It is only a spirit of dedication on our part that can bring about the economic take-off without violence and within the context of a democratic society. It is clear therefore that both classes and masses, which means the nation as a whole, need to be inspired by something more than merely economic motivation. It is only the vision of a new society enticing us into the future that can give us the will and the vigour to work and save in the present.

Even in a capitalist society, economic development had drawn dynamism in its earlier stages from something more than material reward as the motivating factor for its capitalist builders. The non-material element has been a stronger and more conscious factor in the motivation of the communist task forces that have led the communist societies on the path of economic development. In the case of a democratic society, such as India believes in trying to build, the non-material incentive has to play a far more purposive and dynamic role, especially for its better-equipped or better-advantaged classes, than has been the case either in the capitalist or communist experiments in successful economic development.

What we need in India today for solving our economic problem is the building of a national will for the purpose. We often talk of national integration and of emotional integration as urgent national requirements. What we must also remember is the need for a national will for economic development. National will means national discipline. National discipline has to be both individual and collective. As individuals, we have to work hard, save more, and be ready to compromise, if not actually give up, our personal or sectional or group claims in the larger public interest. Functioning collectively, as government and otherwise, we have to concentrate on production and productivity, capital formation and investment, science and technology, and the full utilization of both material and human resources in the collective interest. We must become obsessed with economic development; and both sleeping and waking, we have to concentrate on when, how, and how soon we can raise the rate of economic growth.

Behind it all must be the vision of this new society of social justice and mass welfare that alone can call forth the national will and elicit the national discipline without which there can be no massive development by consent. In concrete terms, this means that for a period of about ten years or so, the nation shall refrain from internal bickerings, strife, and conflicts that weaken the national will for economic development. It means abstention from strikes, lockouts, *gheraoes*, hartals and agitations and allowing nothing that slows down or reduces or halts production. In turn this means that the working of government at all levels and of the economic machinery in all sectors will be permeated by a sense of sympathy and understanding on the part of the better-off for the worse-off, quick and speedy removal of just grievances before they take articulation and ugly shape, and the estab lishment of the rule of social justice and the moral law in place of personal aggrandizement and jungle practices.

Hard work, austere living, increased savings, responsible investment, discipline, collective effort and an overwhelming sense of personal involvement in national uplift—these are the conditions that alone can bring about the needed economic growth consistent with democracy, non-violence, the rule of law, and traditional Indian values. We were greatly fortunate in India for having had in our midst a man of vision and faith who was born on our soil, lived and moved among its masses and led the country to freedom, with love in his heart, God on his lips, and non-violence in his hands. The country has to deserve Mahatma Gandhi. I know it is not easy but I know also that we can do it if only we try hard enough.

In the last analysis, the problem of development for a vast and poor country like India that wants to function within the constraints of a working democracy is not just one of economics. It is much more a problem of character, of ethics, of national discipline, and a national will. Ultimately, the spirit moves where matter fails, and it is this spirit and spirituality that we must invoke in our people if we want to cross the economic barrier.

CHAPTER VIII

DEFENCE AND DEVELOPMENT

When a backward economy in the process of development is also an independent nation, it is concerned not only with development but also with the defence of its territory. When such a developing economy is actually confronted by foreign aggression on its soil, as we have been in India, not only do the resources available for development immediately get eroded by the costs of defensive war, but in addition, its resources for development in the future get further eroded by the additional expenditure it has to incur on a continuing basis because of the permanent increase it has to make to its defence personnel and equipment for preventing, and if necessary, meeting any further foreign aggression it may be subjected to in the future. This means in turn that defence and development both constitute inroads on the national product available for consumption, and therefore, an increase in the magnitude of the savings that the nation has to mobilize both from current income and increments to current income accruing from development. It also implies that the total of these two will be less, as defence expenditure, being unproductive, will not result in increments to national income, while the reduction in development outlay will correspondingly diminish the magnitude of the increment that will accrue from development. The challenge of development for a backward economy like ours thus becomes greater because of the combination of defence with development.

To meet this added challenge, it is necessary for the nation to cultivate both determination and discipline. We have to sink all our petty little differences, resist all stimuli, from wherever they emanate, to the parochial, the communal or the sub-national elements that may still persist in our sub-conscious impulses, and unite as one entity, one nation, and one people. Unity and a sense of common belonging is needed not only in action but also in thought and word. This is the time when all groups in the country, whether political, religious, linguistic or otherwise, should treat each other with generosity and affection, vie with each other in giving rather than taking and build up the invisible bonds that constitute the steel frame of an enduring nation. This cannot be done, however, without discipline.

The discipline required has to show itself in strengthening the willingness to acquire the skills needed for defence and development and working hard and still harder for implementing this willingness. It has also to show itself in every-day life in indifference to petty motivations, tolerance of ways of life different from one's own and, willingness to put up with restraints, austerities, and hardships in order to mobilize the nation's resources for the nation's defence. It is this national will that we must evolve and it is only through such national determination and discipline that we can consciously give flesh and bone to the national will. No power on earth can crush a nation when it discovers its national will and steels itself to implement it with discipline and determination.

The second element in the price that we have to pay for defence with development is in terms of our current and expected standards of consumption. The country has to realize that defence requires resources and while defence also means development, the development will be of a kind that will not mean more consumption. Even in the richest of countries, defence always means diversion of resources from civilian needs to military requirements. In a country like ours, there is no escaping this diversion. True, we can increase the size of the national cake by more determined and better planned utilization of our vast resources of manpower, but the first charge on the increase will be for defence and not for consumption. All of us, civilians and non-combatants, have to adopt austere standards in our consumption levels and patterns. Many things we would like to have we have to postpone for the time being, for we have to release resources for defence and development connected with defence.

It would be a good thing if every one of us were to impose a voluntary cut in our levels of monthly expenditure, quite apart from the cuts that government may impose on our incomes by enhanced taxation. It would be an even better thing if those of us whose incomes have given us a good standard of living so far, were now to impose a voluntary ceiling on our monthly expenditure as long as the emergency lasts and our defence is not strong enough to deter covetous neighbours from even thinking of aggression, let alone acting upon it.

It was Mahatma Gandhi who talked of a ceiling on individual incomes; and it was he who took to the loin cloth in order that he may share the poverty of those who had the privilege to be his fellow countrymen. I am not suggesting that we must all take to the loin cloth or lead the life of *fakirs* or *sadhus*. But I do suggest that we can give up luxuries, comforts and perhaps even conventional needs and function as a civilian army ready to give the needed support to the men on the battle front. Only thus can the physical resources in skills and materials be released without which our armed forces, however, brave and willing to die, would not be able successfully to defend their motherland.

It is not enough to cut down our monthly expenditure and reduce civilian demands upon the economy. It is also necessary to transfer our savings to government for financing its defence and development effort. Otherwise, we run the risk of inflation, headlong rise in the prices of essential articles, and threat to civilian morale, especially of our workers in the fields and the factories. We have to save more; and we have to make these savings available for the defence effort. It is true that a nation of low income individuals does not have much capacity to save.

But this is in the context of peace and routine activity. When a nation has to fight for its very survival, then our concept of savings as surplus must undergo a radical change. Even as a poor family with a sub-standard level of consumption finds, nevertheless, the surplus to give an extra feed to its infant or ailing member, so must a poor nation find a surplus for feeding its soldiers with the equipment that they need. The savings I am talking about are not the classical savings that are either involuntary or are deliberately created to go into investment that will yield a handsome monetary profit. The savings I am talking about in the current context are not for investment, personal reward, or aggrandizement. They are for national survival and for individual survival in so far as nationality and values go to make up their share of the individual. Savings for defence and development therefore do not constitute a surplus over consumption. They take rank with consumption and indeed even claim priority over all unnecessary and non-functional consumption.

It is only when we take this view of savings that we can find the resources necessary for the defence effort and find it in a way that will avoid a stab in the back by way of inflation. All can take part in this effort, not only the rich but also the poor, and not only the old and the middle aged but also the young and the adolescent, including even the tender children of school-going age. It is a hard price to pay, but the price has to be paid, for the issues at stake are beyond all price.

A third component in the price we have to pay for defence and development is the surrender, to the maximum possible extent, of our dependence upon imports and foreign sources. In other words, we have to adopt and implement the principle of self-reliance. This should apply not only to military but also to civil requirements. Self-reliance is a difficult concept. It does not necessarily mean domestic production of everything that we need; but it does mean the ability to pay in foreign exchange for what we are not able produce at home. It means, therefore, not only import substitution but also export promotion. It also means giving up our reliance on foreign aid unless we can get it on terms that do not constitute or even suggest any pressure on us to change our domestic or foreign policies. In any case, self-reliance must mean the giving up of P.L. 480 imports and the implementation of self-sufficiency in food. It certainly means a considerable reduction in our dependence upon foreign aid for our economic development in terms of both project imports and maintenance imports.

All this is going to mean a tremendous effort on the part of our farmers, our industrial workers, our entrepreneurs, our scientists and research workers, and our civil servants. It means duplicating, designing, and improvizing, and this has to be done not only for equipment but also for processes in order to reduce the load on scarce materials. It also means change in producer preference and consumer preferences, and will involve having to do for some time with the second best, provided it has functional efficiency. Self-reliance will also involve changes in Plan priorities with possibly adverse effects on immediate consumption in regard to non-food and non-basic articles of essential necessity. It is not that we have not been pursuing a policy of self-reliance so far in our economic planning. But the pace has been slow and we have been doing it without causing any strain or distress in regard to immediate requirements. Now, we have to step up the pace, as self-reliance has become more urgent in terms of both time and extent in the context of defence with development. The price we have to pay for this haste is a part of the price to be paid for national survival.

Last, but not least among the components of the price to be paid for defence and development, is a much-needed change in the motivation of work, savings and investment. It may be all right in peace time to talk of incentives for every extra bit of work or saving that is needed for development and to give these incentives in monetary form and for the personal benefit of individual participants. But against the present background of emergency and the consequent need for acceleration of defence and related development without incurring the self-defeating risk of inflation, we have to think more seriously of non-monetary and non-personal motivations for the required extra effort. I believe that this change in motivation is not beyond the pale of practical politics; but it will not come unless the lead comes from those who occupy strategic positions in the economy and enjoy incomes far in excess of those earned by the rest of their countrymen.

Equality of sacrifice is the basic bond that enables a

nation at war to rise to the full heights of its potentialities. When our youth have made and are willing to make the supreme sacrifice on the battle field, how can we who remain behind the front, think in terms of economic incentives and extra rewards for every bit of extra work that we do? This is the question that the non-combatants who are required to contribute their extra bit to the defence effort, have to ask themselves. On their answer will depend the measure of success that the nation can achieve in facing this twin challenge of defence and development.

CHAPTER IX

NATIONALISM, DEMOCRACY AND DEVELOPMENT

From what has been said earlier in this brief volume, our problems of development are by no means solved. In fact, the real questions that confront us, both as a nation and as a people, have only just begun to emerge. It is true that India is a nation, a sovereign State, a democracy, and has declared her goal to be the achievement of a socialist society. But all this constitutes no more than a framework. The real question is, has India become emotionally and spiritually integrated into one nation? Has she established the conditions for the enduring stability of her sovereign status? Has she really learnt the art of successfully operating a political democracy? And, finally, have our people, both leaders and masses, properly grasped the idea of a socialist society and actively resolved to bring it into operation. These are vital questions and they need urgent answering.

Take first the question of emotional integration. It is comparatively easy for a people living under a common political jurisdiction to attach themselves emotionally to each other and feel themselves as one nation, when they have a common language, a common religion, a common history, and common habits and customs in respect of food, clothing and the like. It is very much more difficult for a country like ours to do so because of the vastness of its area, the multitude of its people, and the diversity of its languages, religions, habits, and regional histories. It is true that we have an underlying unity of culture but even this unity has got diluted by the cultural diversities of its major religious and linguistic groupings.

No doubt, resistance to British rule, emergence of an all India political upper class of English-knowing people, and leadership of the Congress under Mahatma Gandhi gave us a certain measure of emotional integration and helped not only in the winning of Independence but also in maintaining it so far. But these factors are tending to disappear with the efflux of time. British rule has gone, the English-knowing all-India political class is being fast replaced by diverse and regional Indian language groups, the Congress is beginning to lose its positive national appeal, and the memory of Mahatma Gandhi has started dimming in the public consciousness. It is true that we have a great unifying force in the person of Shrimati Indira Gandhi but it is also a fact that no other person with an equivalent emotional appeal is visible on the Indian national horizon. Emotional integration of the type that has made the British nation, for example, is still to be achieved in India.

In the only three other countries in the world, with the vastness of area and largeness of numbers that we have in India, positive steps have been taken and in a purposive manner to achieve the emotional integrity so necessary for constituting a nation. The USSR and China have brought the powerful influence of a monolithic and dedicated communist party, with millions of active workers and supported by a totalitarian political administration, in order to build up this feeling of emotional integration in their peoples. The United States, on the other hand, has followed an active policy of "100 per cent American" and used the "melting pot" theory to make one nation out of the diverse religious and racial groups of immigrants that constitute so many of its citizens.

We, in India, do not want to have a totalitarian system; nor can the Indian Congress Party of today be compared either in its spirit of dedication and discipline or in the number of its active workers, to the communist parties either of the Soviet Union or of China. At the same time, the diversities of language and religion that we have in India are a historical heritage and do not, therefore, lend themselves to the type of pressure and control that the United States could exert on its heterogenous mass of European immigrants. Our problems, therefore are infinitely more difficult than those of the three other great countries which are comparable to us in size and number.

Closely linked with the problem of emotional integration is also that of securing the conditions for an enduring stability of our position as a sovereign State. Once we achieve emotional integration and every citizen of India gets permeated with a feeling of Indian nationality, we shall have also secured the conditions for the enduring stability of our State. The rest is largely a matter of administration and governmental efficiency. But the cardinal factor is emotional integration. Once India becomes a real nation, no power on earth, neither cajolery nor trickery nor armaments, can destroy it. Governments can be overthrown, but not peoples; countries can be overrun, but not nations. Once we feel and function as a nation, our political stability can be menaced only from within; and there will no internal menace either, once we achieve active political democracy and secure real economic justice for our masses.

How do we set about bringing this emotional integration?

The most enduring way in which we can do this is by knowledge of and pride in the past, knowledge of and respect for
one another, active participation in common undertakings,
and mutual aid in the solution of each other's difficulties.
First of all, all of us who can read and write and the rest of
us who can neither read nor write, but can certainly both see
and hear, must be made aware of the long and continuous
history of India's one cultural entity. The great spiritual
sons and daughters of India have, through the ages, spread
their influence throughout the country, irrespective of the
regional area from which they came or of the linguistic group
to which they belonged. Rama and Krishna, Buddha and
Mahavira, Sankara and Ramanuja, Madhava and Chaitanya,
Basava and Tukaram, Kabir and Nanak, Meera and Tulsidas,
Dayanand and Ram Mohan, Ramakrishna and Vivekananda,
Aurobindo and Gandhi and now Jawaharlal and Vinobha—
these are the possessions of India and belong to all regions
of India and to all languages of India.

This very knowledge, and with it the legitimate sense of
pride and therefore of responsibility it is bound to evoke,
will itself go a long way to produce a sense of emotional
identity among our people. It is not enough, however,
merely to know and feel proud of our common cultural heritage. It is equally important for us to become aware, in a
literally physical sense, of the richness and variety of our
geography, and get acquainted with the looks and manners,
problems and aspirations of the many groups of men and
women who inhabit different parts of our country. In the
old days, it was the *thirtha yatra* that made this possible. We
have to find a modern substitute for this ancient pilgrimage
to the holy places, by the new pilgrimage that Nehru has
talked about where new India's economy is being forged and
to the regions whose inhabitants are now seeking a new unity

in their Indian nationality. Every university and college should establish a sisterhood relationship with another university or college separated from it by both distance and language, and offer and receive hospitality for selected members of one another. Each university should open departments of Indian culture, including art and literature, and offer compulsory courses on the thesis that "unity in diversity" which constitutes the essence of Indian nationality. It is also necessary that instruction be imparted in our colleges and universities on the main tenets of the principal religions that are professed in India, and the essential unity that underlies their approach to God and their attitude to man. "एकं सत् विप्रा बहुधा वदन्ति" said our ancient sages. It is this tolerance, this mutual respect for each other's faith, this brotherhood of all religions and the supremacy of religion as such, that forms the soul of India. How, then, can we neglect religion in our education if our objective is to build a united India by removing possible barriers to the emotional integration of our people? A secular State does not mean an anti-religious state. And religion can never disappear from India. Therefore, let us restore religion to its proper place in the educational system of India. "अहिंसा परमो धर्मः" said Mahatma Gandhi; and the mighty truth of that simple statement should echo and re-echo round the rooms and corridors of our universities and colleges, and then permeate the entire country through the agency of our student community.

Unity, however, is not merely a matter either of thought or of feeling. It is also a process, a fact that emerges out of the very nature of one's activity and organic growth, which should blend almost unconsciously with the development of the country. Active participation in common undertakings and mutual aid in regional projects are the means through which we can generate national unity as a process of India's economic and social growth. For this purpose, it is essential that great undertakings of a national character, such as our mighty irrigation and power projects or our industrial plants in the public sector or other national undertakings in the economic field, should provide the opportunity for active participation of Indians from all parts of the country, irrespective of which region a particular project may be located.

Positive steps must also be taken to see that this opportunity is actually availed of by our people. Thus, our people from the south, east and west could have been recruited to take active part in the construction of the Bhakra Nangal project; similarly, those from the north, the south, and the west in the Damodar Valley project. This active participation could have taken place either in kind or in cash, and in any case, it should have included visits, study, knowledge, and appreciation.

Similarly, groups and cadres could be organized in each state which will offer their services to another state in the implementation of such of their regional projects of mass appeal as can efficiently make use of these services. Thus, Bombay teams could work on Bihar projects and Bihar teams on Bombay projects; while Bombay, Bihar, Bengal and the rest of our eighteen States could send teams to work on all-India projects. Such teams, supplemented by camps and study tours, would go a long way in promoting inter-State contacts, breaking down language barriers, building emotional attachments, and creating the feeling that all Indians are but one people and that India is one nation.

In this task, our universities and colleges can play an important role. They can each set up special units for the purpose of giving select bodies of students the opportunity to take an active part in the great task of nation-building which we call our Five Year Plans. Each of these action units can establish contact with corresponding units in other states and chalk out a programme for mutual exchange of services.

It is not sufficient, however, either for our evolution as a nation or for the enduring stability of our sovereign status that we achieve emotional integration through our history, our culture, and our inter-State contacts. It is even more important that we secure the proper working of political democracy in India and resolutely march forward towards the goal of a socialist society for our people. Political democracy does not mean merely exercizing the right of voting and selecting any particular political party for forming the government. It involves the far more difficult and continuous task of understanding and practising the obligations of active citizenship.

Citizenship means that we are prepared, each one of us, to spend a part of our time understanding the problems that constitute the subject of governmental policy and action, bringing the light of reason and the warmth of brotherhood to the consideration of these problems, promoting discussion and avoiding dogmatism, and, finally, showing readiness to make a personal contribution towards the implementation of policies and programmes that are in the public interest. There can be no passive citizenship in a democracy, especially one such as ours, which is still in a state of infancy and yet is called upon to undertake the most gigantic tasks of national reconstruction. No genuine citizen can leave everything to the government or think that he has no individual responsibility for the running of his country.

This conception of active citizenship and, even more, its translation into positive action, is not something that will spring spontaneously either in India or elsewhere. The seed needs to be planted, it needs to be nurtured, and it needs to be sustained. No agency is more appropriate for this purpose than the university and the college. It is the student who can best understand both the privilege and the responsibility of citizenship in a political democracy and it is in the college and the university that he must be given the opportunity to learn the habit of active citizenship.

I would therefore encourage the formation of political clubs and multi-party parliaments in each college and university. These should constitute not only centres for discussion where both reason and emotion can have play, but should also have active programme, which will give, to such of their members as so choose opportunities for making their individual contribution towards the implementation of one or other of the many accepted objectives of our democratic republic. Students are the natural vehicle for communication of the ideas of citizenship and are also, in many ways, the natural initiators of the practice of citizenship.

I am not suggesting for a moment that political parties should start using student groups for party purposes; that would indeed be a tragedy. The political clubs and college parliaments that I speak about must be completely free from the control both of political parties and academic administrations. They can have contacts with and seek advice from both, but operation and control must be entirely theirs. Only thus can ideas of citizenship grow among those who constitute the natural leaders of the community and through them envelope the entire land. It is student discussion and student activity that can create the feeling of citizenship and promote the working of democracy, not just syllabuses and lectures in citizenship.

Students, though a leading section in the world of youth,

do not constitute more than a minor portion of its number. Non-student youth, whether employed or unemployed or working on their own, constitute more than 95 per cent of the age-group 16 to 21 and form what may be called the proletariat of the youth world in so far as hardly any attention is paid either to their cultural or their sports needs. What is even more important in the context of this chapter is the neglect they suffer in regard to their education in values, or a reasoned understanding of the democratic process and the implications it gives rise to in terms of attitudes and skills.

Special attention requries to be paid therefore, to the problem of non-student youth and it was a progressive step on the part of the Prime Minister to have redesignated the Ministry of Education as the Ministry of Education and Youth Services in 1969. The problem of non-student youth thus got official recognition, a National Youth Welfare Board was constituted and concrete programmes drawn up for youth welfare and involvement in national development. It is a matter for regret that, when the central council of Ministers was reconstituted after the mid-term poll early this year, youth services got lost in the process and the Ministry of Education has acquired instead the department of Social Welfare. It is hoped that the omission was either inadvertent or accounted for by amalgamating it with social welfare.

In any case, there can be no doubt that non-student youth constitute a dynamic element in our society both by their numbers and the energy natural to their age group. If steps are not taken to tackle their problems and give them the necessary orientation in values, skills and attitudes relevant for development under democracy, they may well become an obstacle in the way of a peaceful and orderly working of democracy in spite of any progressive lead given by the educated youth who have been through colleges and universities.

Political democracy is, however, not enough. We must also have justice, both social and economic. We have to establish a socialist society in India. But this must not be a socialist society nurtured on foreign soil and just transplanted on our land. We have too long a history, our traditions and values are too rich, and our thoughts and reactions too mature, for our people to accept the role of pale imitators of foreign creeds. Socialism for us cannot be a mere economic doctrine nor a particular interpretation of history. It is not Marx or Lenin or Mao that can provide the basic force for the socialist ideal in India. Our socialism derives its base from the deep recesses of our spiritual heritage. The universality of the *Atman*, before whose identity fades away all claims for privileges and justifications for differences, is the spiritual charter for our socialist ideal of equality.

It is true that this charter has been misread in the past and misinterpreted in our history when applied to the actual relations of human beings to one another. Casteism, feudalism, tyranny, all these have flourished in India, and have not yet disappeared from our sight. But the seed is pure and can still be dug out from our soil. For those of us who are Hindus, there is no question of the equality of men before God. God is in man, and all men have in them a spark of divinity. How then can we claim special privileges for some men and life-long disabilities for many others when all of them have the same *Atman*, the same God, the same urge, the same spirit? That is why a great prophet-patriot like Swami Vivekananda proclaimed from the house tops that his religion taught him that service to man constitutes the worship of God. That is why Gandhiji talked of *daridra narayana*, and Vinobhaji today talks of all property as belonging to God and, therefore, calls for *Bhoodan*, *Sampattidan* and *daans* of other kinds.

The basis of our socialism is, therefore, spiritual. The method for attaining it therefore, has to be spiritual too. Hence our linking-up of non-violence with the achievement of a socialist society. Our armoury, therefore, is not hatred but love, not dictatorship but democracy, not revolution but evolution, not coercion but consent. This is Indian socialism. Like socialism elsewhere, our socialism also seeks to achieve equality and justice; likewise it envisages an institutional reorganization of both society and government for the implementation of the socialist way. What is unique about our socialism is its Indian origin, its spiritual base, and its non-violent approach.

It is important that our students and teachers should ponder well and deeply on the meaning of the socialist society that we have decided on as our goal. Having done so, they should spread the light far and wide among people. Also they must learn and then transmit the key to the achievement of this society. The key is neither just legislation nor mere extension of governmental activity. The key to Indian socialism is essentially an individual key, the attitude each individual should adopt towards men and property, in fact, to life itself. It is only when millions of men and women in India adopt the socialist attitude in their personal life and conduct, that India can truly achieve a socialist society. Hence, the importance of universities and colleges in the achievement of socialism. To me, universities are not merely centres of learning nor recruiting grounds for employment. Our universities have also a vital role to play in the rejuvenation of our nation, the restoration of her glory, and the maintenance of her freedom. It is not the volume of learning but the nature of the attitude that they instil in their students that will determine the real utility of universities and colleges in India. It is the attitude that the student develops during his college years that will shape his future conduct and conversation; and if these are to be worthy of the university, it must acknowledge and play its role as a nation-building agency. I think, therefore, it is high time that those in charge of university education in India stepped down from their ivory tower, ceased thinking of themselves as persons unconcerned with the political, social and economic reality against which they function, and started working as trustees in charge of one of the most important agencies for the building of the Indian nation and the Indian people. Let them pay heed to the experience of other parts of the world and realize that even their cherished concepts of "academic freedom" and "learning for the sake of learning" can flourish only in a free, democratic, and just society. And in the establishment and maintenance of such a society, the younger generation can play its essential role, only if the universities stimulate and strengthen in their pupils the attitude appropriate for the purpose. Only then will it be possible for the graduates of this or of any other university in India to be addressed with the wise and immortal words of the Buddha:

चरत भिक्क तारिकम्
(Move on, move on, Oh, Bhikkus, bringing wealth and happiness to the people).

To these I would add: बहुजन हिताय बहुजन सुखाय
बहुजन रक्षणाय बहुजन समत्वाय
freely translating them thus,
"bringing protection to the nation and equality to its people."

Our youth and especially our students, both graduates and would-be graduates, are our country's natural missionaries and on them rests the burden not only of discovering India but also of looking after India. In the glorious words of Swami Vivekananda:

"Let us all work hard, my brethren, this is no time for sleep. On our work depends the coming of the India of the future. She is there, ready, waiting. She is only sleeping. Arise, and awake and see her seated here, on her eternal throne, rejuvenated, more glorious than she ever was—this motherland of ours. And may He who is the Siva of the Saivites, the Vishnu of the Vaishnavites, the Karma of the Karmis, the Buddha of the Buddhists, the Jina of the Jains, the Jehovah of the Christians and the Jews, the Allah of the Mohammedans, the Lord of every sect, the Brahman of Vedantists, He the all-pervading whose glory has been known only in this land—may He bless us, may He help us, may He give strength unto us, energy unto us, to carry this idea into practice. May that which we have listened to and studied become food to us, may it become strength in us, may it become energy in us to help each other: may we, the teacher and the taught, not be jealous of each other."

CHAPTER X

VALUES AND DEVELOPMENT—
THE ROLE OF UNIVERSITIES

While India has taken up the Herculean task of economic development alongside defence preparedness, and within the constraints of a parliamentary democracy, there is insufficient appreciation of the human effort involved. The values relevant for facilitating this process are not yet emerging in sufficient measure in India. In fact, by all accounts, outdated and anti-development values like casteism, groupism, communalism, regionalism, linguism and other anachronistic social attitudes are continuing to exist, if not also expanding, in our country. Old prejudices are actually gathering strength, and new prejudices are now getting added to their number. At the same time, old values are dying, but new ones are not emerging in their place.

India is in the throws of a social and cultural revolution that seems to have caught the elite by the wrong foot and threatens to undo the great work that Mahatma Gandhi started, of fashioning a harmonious, non-violent and compassionate society dedicated to the service of *daridra narayan* and deriving its strength from faith in God and love for all living creatures. It is at a time like this in a nation's history, when economic development rings out the old and rings in the new, that the educated classes face their greatest challenge as leaders of society. Our educated youth and especially our student community constitute a part of this class. On them is going to fall the mantle of leadership and the challenge that goes with it for building soundly and firmly on the foundations that Gandhiji laid, rather than build their houses on the sand that glitters so abundantly in contemporary India.

What is it that society seeks in the educated man? Knowledge, a scientific temper, the right attitude to work, an awareness of the society round about him, especially of its needs and its limitations, courtesy, compassion, discipline, and a pride that combines humility in personal behaviour with high endeavour in functional activity—these are the traits that one seeks to find in educated men. I may be accused of setting out an ideal list of attributes, and indulging in an utopian exercise, but how otherwise can we create the good society that we all profess such anxiety to see established in our country?

Many factors have a role in the creation of these attributes. The educated man not only influences the society he lives in but is also influenced by it. The university and the values it imparts are, perhaps, the most important among the factors that influence the make-up of the educated men. It may be worthwhile therefore, to look at our universities and see what role they are playing in providing their pupils with the values and the qualities of leadership that the country so badly requires for facing the challenge of the political, economic, social, and cultural revolution that has started in contemporary India.

The post-independence and post-planning period has seen a large increase in the number of our universities, the number of colleges that constitute or are affiliated to these universities, and the number of pupils that are attending their courses. The quantity has certainly increased but one is not sure about the nature of the change that has taken place in quality. There are complaints about falling academic standards about which it is possible to hold differing views. There can be no difference of opinion, however, about the deterioration in student discipline, and the growing indifference of the student community towards knowledge for its own sake. Reading habits are declining and intellectual curiosity is on the wane. Traditional values are at a discount, irrespective of their relevance to modern Indian problems, and Indian culture is given way before a polyglot caricature of western culture. Competition is taking the place of co-operation, and the economic motive is becoming ascendant. The rat race so familiar to an industrial civilization is on in our own country.

Social awareness and social passion are a rarity rather than a familiar phenomenon, and the gulf that separates the classes from the masses is widening not only in terms of economic conditions and opportunities, but also in terms of comprehension, understanding, and communication. To the sensitive among the elite and educated class, the salt seems to be losing its flavours, and there is no knowing what response one is going to make to the growing, and indeed menacing, challenge of the transition in India. Unless one holds on to the right values and lets them guide our personal conduct, all the progress we are making with our planned economy may prove to have been in vain and the good society we seek may well elude our quest.

What are these right values that we need in India? To begin with, we have to nurse our infant democracy and let it strike deep and strong roots in the Indian soil and its people. Democracy can succeed only if the educated classes who provide leadership, develop respect for the masses, understanding of their problems, and show readiness to subordinate their individual or class welfare to collective and mass welfare. Above all, it is important to ensure that issues are fairly and squarely placed before the people, that nothing is done either to confuse or mislead them, and that their positive co-operation and participation is secured in the task of government.

Every university student should be given the opportunity to learn about democracy, its props and its pitfalls, and the rules of the game within which alone a democratic system can operate with success. Objective data on the actual working of Indian democracy at all its levels—local, state and national—should be available for study by the student community, and free intellectual discussion should be encouraged with spokesmen of different political parties. It is not necessary for students to take active part in politics; but they must have an understanding of political events and programmes and be encouraged to apply logic and analysis to political questions instead of being swayed by rhetoric and passion born of prejudice. Debates, study circles, and seminars should be encouraged on political problems, but it should be the business of someone in a responsible position in the university to see that real discussion take places, pros and cons are fairly set out in each case, and slogans and catchwords are not used to take the place of logic and argument.

If students do not develop an intellectual interest in politics and an objective understanding of political events during their stay in the university, they will fail to constitute intelligent public opinion when they go out. The result will be either passivity or mere attention to self-interest on the part of the educated classes. Politicians will not have the guidance or deterrance of well-informed and objective public opinion. Slogans, passions, and prejudices will hold sway, and faith in democracy will undergo a gradual erosion that may ulti-

mately expose Indian democracy to the fate that has over-
taken democracy in so many other independent countries of
Asia, Africa, and Latin America. The universities have a
definite role in the defence of democracy by the way in which
they inculcate in their pupils an understanding of democratic
practices, appreciation of democratic values, and intelligent
interest in political problems.

On the economic side, it is important to see that the right
attitude to work is encouraged and that monetary incentives
are not always held up as the sole incentive for economic
activity. We need full appreciation by our student community of the dignity of labour. The relation between income
and work needs to be stressed. The feeling should be cultiva-
ted that unearned income, or income got through specula-
tion, profiteering or other unproductive or anti-social means,
does not have either the flavour or the justification that
attaches to income earned by work and performance of a
legitimate function.

A socialist society does not rest merely upon a framework
of distributional justice; it also presupposes superior productivity. Pride in the efficient preformance of one's work must
be built into the psychology of the student community, as
also a feeling of pride in public property and watchfulness in
its safety and efficiency. A socialist society means a large
public sector; and unless the public sector is productive and
works with efficiency, a socialist society is not likely to succeed. The efficiency of the public sector rests in turn on the
development of a sense of identification by its workers, and
this requires the building up of an appropriate psychological
attitude, which could be done at the university stage more
easily.

A socialist society also means regulation, controls, and an
extensive bureaucracy. If these are to operate without inhibit-

ing initiative or stimulating corruption, the necessary values and the appropriate psychology have to be built into the curricular and extra-curricular activities and the atmosphere that is a part of the university. Socialism as a way of life for those who belong to the upper strata of society is not easy nor does it come naturally. It requires conviction and culti- vation, both of which are more easily possible for the educated class at the university stage than later. Hence the importance of the role that a university can play in laying the psycholo- gical foundations for a socialist order by the atmosphere it creates and the values it inculcates during the formative years when its students enter and pass through its portals.

The educated classes have also to take into account the new social aspirations and attitudes released by the advent of in- dependence, the establishment of political democracy, the beginnings of industrialization, and planned economic growth. The Constitution has abolished untouchability. Members of Scheduled Castes and Scheduled Tribes enjoy the same political rights as other sections of the Indian people, their representatives sit in the Central Parliament and in State assemblies and special financial and administrative provisions are made for their welfare.

And yet, no one can deny the existence of a profound feel- ing of dissatisfaction among these backward sections of the Indian community. Political rights, constitutional guarantees, and special financial provisions are all right as far as they go, but they do not go far enough. What these classes seek is social recognition. They want status and social acceptance, and they find they are not getting it from the caste Hindus in spite of professions of equality and socialist ideology.

This is especially so in the rural areas, where the bulk of our people live. In how many villages do the caste Hindus share drinking wells with the Harijans? How far have intimate social contacts been established between caste Hindus and others in our universities and colleges? In what way is the educated man showing in his daily life, his acceptance of the principle of social equality? What are we doing in the universities to expound the ideology of the casteless, classless, and socialist society which is now presumably the nation's accepted objective?

Have the universities thrown up bands of young men and women in the post-independence period who have made it their business to fight social distinctions, social discrimination, and social inequalities? Is the university helping to awaken the social conscience of the individual student? We all talk of social work and social service societies functioning in colleges and universities. How far have these societies permeated the life of the student community? Do the poor and the lowly, either in the villages or in the urban areas recognize in the university student their special friend who understands their difficulties, is moved by their distress, and would like to do something constructive to help them? Do we have any movement in our universities like the American Peace Corps initiated by the late President Kennedy? Is the social gap narrowing in India? Are our universities helping to create in the student mind the picture of an integrated Indian society shorn of its hierarchical distinction and its hereditary divisions and telling him in what way he as an individual, can help in getting nearer the realization of such a society?

These questions have only to be asked to get an immediate answer. What needs to be emphasized is that a social revolution is taking place, and unless we, who are the products of universities, take the lead in the march towards social equality, we will be swept aside and others who take our place, may not have had the advantage of a university education.

The country is also undergoing a cultural revolution. The educated classes are fast losing their faith in the traditional forms of religion and in the traditional values of religion. At the same time, no other religion or religious values are taking their place; nor is any attempt being made to remould old religious forms to suit modern requirements while retaining their mass appeal and especially the values they stand for. What I am saying is with particular reference to the religious community to which I belong, namely, the Hindus. While religion is flying out of the window of the educated modern Hindu, other cults and superstitions, including a naive belief in astrology, charms and the like, are taking their place. The educated Hindu's loss of faith in his traditional religion is not even being compensated by the substitution of a robust atheism having its roots in humanitarianism and compassion. On the contrary, his superstitions are increasing and with it his fears and sense of insecurity, which his loss of faith no longer enables him to cope with.

Thanks to the abnormal and unnatural importance attached by the elite of India to the use of English as the medium of instruction, the university student is no longer interested in acquiring command over the language or languages which are the repository of his cultural and spiritual heritage. Nor is he able to acquire that command over the English language which will make it his own and enable him to use it not only for passing his examinations and holding conversations, official and otherwise, but also as an instrument for acquiring and expanding his universe of knowledge. His command over the English language is not good enough and he struggles to acquire just enough competence to answer his papers and pass his examination, and, too often, he fails.

The linguistic hurdle he has to cross makes him concentrate on guide books, notes, and other aids to memorizing.

Knowledge for its own sake becomes a secondary consideration; he fails to develop a living interest in the subjects he studies in the university and ceases to be a student once he has passed out of the portals of his university. The major objectives of university education, namely, the development of, interest in, and capacity for acquiring further knowledge in his subjects eludes his grasp. All too soon after his graduation, and in far too many cases, university education gets to be only an interlude and he lapses back into the category of the less educated, the knowledge he acquired during his college days getting dimmer with time as he fails to keep it up to date by further reading.

We have yet to grasp the full significance of the loss caused by the use of an alien language as the medium of instruction at the university stage. Meanwhile, what is clear is that this creates a further gap between the classes and the masses. Our university graduates are losing contact with their own tradition and cultural values, nor are they acquiring the basic values and culture of those whose language they use as their medium of instruction. They do not write in English because they do not have enough command over that language; nor do they write in their own language as their media of instruction have not been their mother-tongues. Indian languages are therefore failing to grow socially and scientifically rich in the way European languages have grown over the last hundred years or so. As a natural consequence, modern knowledge and attitudes are not spreading out among the people at large and the country is left with a gaping cultural vacuum which its educated classes are not able to fill.

This may seem a harsh indictment of our university education today. But I do feel strongly that our nation today is in a crisis of character; and the only way in which we can meet it successfully is through man-making and character-building education. Of course, education has to serve the needs of the economy, and our universities must produce the skills and the attitudes, as well as the research that is necessary for meeting the needs of our planned economy and accelerating the rate of our economic growth.

But we are not planning only for a material civilization. As Sri Shankaracharya of Kanchi has said, "We must be concerned not only with the *standard of living* but also with the *standard of life*." We have proclaimed aloud our faith in human and spiritual values. We want to create a classless and castless society based on truth and non-violence. We want to develop a socialist order. We are proud of our independence. We want to combine the best in our national past with the best in the global present so that our future will be based, to use Acharya Vinoba Bhave's language, on science and spirituality.

These are values, and values need to be expounded, they need to be taught, and they need to be integrated with our daily lives. Universities are the true repositories of values, and they alone can perform the function of expounding values and integrating them into the lives of those who pass through their gates. We in the universities have therefore to ask ourselves what values we are integrating into the student community who form our trust and charge.

All our universities have mottos which are drawn usually from our ancient writings and embody values that have come down from the ages. What are we doing about giving meaning and reality to these values in the eyes of our students? How far are we preparing our educated classes to meet the challenge of the crisis in character that faces our nation today? While the nation must rightly go forward in its quest for material wealth and abolition of mass poverty, cannot we also retain our spiritual outlook and make it richer by combining with it the scientific spirit which is the contribution of modern civilization? The masses must have bread before they can think of anything else; but the classes who have bread, and, in some cases, also butter if not jam as well, can surely think in terms of trusteeship, sacrifice, renunciation and service—all virtues that have an honoured place in our national heritage.

The educated man should be distinguished for holding the right values, and it is the university which imparts education. It is therefore in the university that the student seeks to acquire values. Are our universities fulfilling this function today? On the answer to this question and the action we take as a follow-up of the answer, will depend the prospects of the new society we are trying to build and especially the methods that will be employed, violent or non-violent, to bring it into existence. Our universities can rise to the challenge only if they cease to be either ivory towers or mere architects of material values, and take on the task of imbuing their students with the values that will make them good men and good women and thus enable them to build up the good society beloved of the seers, sung by the poets, and, in our own lifetime, immortalized by the life and teachings of Mahatma Gandhi.

CHAPTER XI

MASS EDUCATION AND DEVELOPMENT

We have been discussing the special role of university educated youth in dealing with the problems of Indian development in the context of parliamentary democracy, the leadership that they can give to the rest of the community, and the part that universities can play in training them for this task. But university education is not co-extensive with education nor is Indian economic development only a function of the values and attitudes of graduates and would-be graduates. The totality of workers and peasants who constitute the masses are also involved in the process and they are not just passive participants who follow the example set by the elite. They also have an autonomous being in the values, attitudes and skills they acquire or cultivate. In this, they are influenced by the education they receive. Thus primary and secondary education constitute important factors in influencing the nature and price of economic development and it is to this aspect of the Indian scene that we turn in this chapter.

Primary and secondary education, even more than university education, has got to be related to economic development both in content and methodology. Apart from those who receive no education at all, more than 90 per cent of those who receive it do not reach the university age, and of these more than 80 per cent do not go beyond the primary stage. It is essential therefore, that education at these stages has a developmental bias and is treated as investment rather than merely as social welfare activity or formal fulfilment of a constitutional directive.

From this point of view, there is no doubt that our educational system is not yielding an appropriate economic return on the expenditure that is being incurred on it. To begin with, a substantial portion of the expenditure we incur on primary education is sheer waste because of the continuing phenomenon of drop-outs that is responsible for only about 50 per cent of those entering the first class actually reaching the fifth class. Those who do not receive primary education for a minimum period of four years—and these account for a majority of the children enrolled in the first class—lapse into illiteracy, even if some of them had managed to acquire literacy; and illiteracy certainly comes in the way of their responding to the opportunities opened out by economic development, let alone adding to these opportunities.

For those who reach the end of the primary stage or even go through the secondary stage, the content and methodology of the education they receive is of crucial relevance for their participation in the development process. Education must increase their productivity; and the incremental contribution that this makes to production must be much more than the expenditure incurred thereon. The productivity orientation referred to is not to be assessed merely in terms of facilitating employment or getting higher wages or salaries in employment.

Our educational system, for historical reasons, has been

linked with the getting of jobs rather than self-employment, with the result that it has been so organized and motivated so as to reduce initiative, self-reliance, and readiness to take risks. And this creates an attitude in the educated man that getting a routine job is the only way of making a living. Whether the remedy lies in altering the atmosphere in schools or in the content of education or in the methods of teaching or in the inclusion of training in manual skills or a combination of all these is a matter for determination by the educational expert. But what is obvious is that there should be a change in the educational system with a view to producing more initiative and self-reliance and a bias towards independent economic activity.

What is needed is the stimulation of qualities such as initiative, imagination, risk-taking, willingness to take on any job, and ability to get on with people. There is also a need for cultivating respect for the dignity of manual labour and not allowing oneself to be lured away by a false sense of status and respectability that is supposed to characterize white collar jobs. If these qualities and attitudes are to be promoted by our educational system, it must get a new orientation by way of basic education, craft education, fundamental education, tool shop practice, manual labour, vocationalization of education or by other radical alterations in the content and methods of teaching.

All this is acknowledged and is a part of the routine official declarations on education, but practice has not followed profession. The pilot projects and the experimentation needed to give content and nationally workable programmes in this direction have been started by the Central Education Ministry a few months back, but one does not know how long it will take before concrete programmes for revolutionizing our educational system come into being in place of the lofty calls and declarations for a revolution in Indian education that are repeatedly being made by those in high political authority. Meanwhile, *ad hoc* measures are being tried and some individual successes have been obtained, but the system as a whole continues to remain out of tune with the skills and psychology needed for massive economic development.

What is not realized is that good education is not cheap education, and development-oriented education is bound to be more expensive than just literacy or academic or memory-centred education, though in terms of returns in developmental efficiency it is actually cheaper. The sooner it is realized that cheap education is ineffective education and that ineffective education is perhaps worse than no education, the sooner will we begin to understand the nature of education as investment.

The fact is that primary education, which is the only education that the masses are likely to get for a long time, has received but little attention in terms of improvement in quality. Even in terms of quantity it commands such a low priority in our planning—in spite of the specific constitutional directive for the implementation of free and compulsory primary education within 10 years of the enactment of the Constitution—which meant by 1961—that at the current rate of progress, even the advent of the 21st century will not see compulsory and free primary education up to the age of 14 in all parts of the country.

Added to this deficiency in regard to primary education, adult illiteracy is another powerful deterrent to economic development. Literacy which was 24 per cent in 1961, has only increased to 30 per cent in 1971. Even this low national average does not give a complete picture of the state of literacy in the country, as it conceals the much lower

percentages of literacy that are prevalent in the rural population and among women in the country as a whole. Illiterate
people are neither motivated nor qualified to make full
use of the facilities created for economic development, whether in the field of agricultural production, co-operative societies, family planning programmes, the adoption of new
techniques in rural or small scale industries or an intelligent
and economic use of credit for increasing production.

It shows the lopsidedness in our centralized planning
that has given so little attention to the increase of literacy
in spite of its developmental stimulus, and except for
Maharashtra, no other state in India has taken up on a mass
scale, the liquidation of illiteracy. It is only within the last
one year that a National Adult Education Board has been
established, literacy targets laid down for a ten-year period,
and pilot projects for a 100 per cent literacy on a district
basis sanctioned for adoption. How these will fare and progress depends upon how the new Government formed at
the Centre after the mid-term poll, continues to pay attention to the liquidation of illiteracy as both a developmental and a social objective.

The spread of literacy alone is not enough to bring about
the utilization of developmental opportunities. Literacy has
to lead to education, the acquisition of at least the rudimen-
tary knowledge of science and technology that an industrial
society requires in the masses of its workers and peasants,
and the creation of the scientiffc temper and industrial discipline so essential for modernizing a backward economy. This
means that facilities should be created for the utilization of
literacy and steps taken for the creation of the needed facilities
for such utilization.

The literacy that is geared to the promotion of economic
development is functional literacy, which means literacy of

the type that can stimulate the will for development and also create the capacity for development. All this involves a massive programme of book production for the neo-literates in the Indian languages and village, towns and district libraries for their circulation. Some attempt in this direction has been started in the last four months but we have a long way to go and much will depend upon the new Planning Commission and the new Central Government as to how far and how fast we go on this road of functional literacy and its utilization by the masses.

Adult literacy and adult education for the masses are also required for the promotion of social development. Social development involves the creation of a progressive social outlook in terms of rationality, attitude to women and to the weaker sections of society, and desire for knowledge. Another important component of a progressive social outlook is the cultivation of the long as against the short view, as society has a continuity extending far beyond the lives of those who compose it at any one moment. This preference for a long view among the masses is particularly essential for a developing society, where the effort of today should be dictated more by the requirements of tomorrow than by the satisfaction of the needs of today.

It will however take some time before we can make literates out of the present many million illiterates in the country and it will also take some time before books and libraries in the required number and location become available for the neo-literates and other educated adults seeking general education in science and culture. Even then, they may not be able to cover all the requirements of continuing education for school drop-outs, neo-literates, and other educated adults.

It would therefore be a good thing if the institution of

the Open University that has now been developed in England is also taken up in our country. Only it should not be confined to university students and correspondence courses for higher education as in England, but extended to cover the rest of the population seeking knowledge to whom reference has been made earlier. In fact, for a vast population like India's, and with our meagre financial resources available for education, it would be more appropriate for India to re-adopt the Open University system to suit the educational requirements of the school drop-outs, the neo-literates, the illiterates, and the educated adults who desire continuing education and make available for them interesting programmes of instruction based on modern science-oriented educational technology, functional technical education, and cultural education. If this suggestion is accepted, it would go a long way in hastening and modernizing the education of the Indian masses and preparing them for responding appropriately to the opportunities opened up by economic development as also enabling them to add to these opportunities. We may now sum up the position in words that we have used elsewhere:

The human factor, which is a most important instrument for the promotion of economic and social development and which simultaneously is the main beneficiary of such development, requires that there is education on a mass scale. This is not possible without adult literacy. Without adult education and adult literacy, it is not possible to have that range and speed of economic and social development that we require, nor is it possible to have that content or quality or tone in our economic and social development that makes it worthwhile in terms of values and welfare. A programme of adult education and adult literacy should therefore take a front place in any programme for economic and social development.

CHAPTER XII

PSYCHOLOGICAL FOUNDATIONS

We lack today that sense of excitement and great endeavour that invigorated us when we were fighting for the restoration of our national freedom. We do not appear to have a feeling of unified purpose, the camaraderie that comes from collective effort seems absent, and personal and selfish ends dominate our activity rather than a spirit of subordination to something larger than our individual selves. Regionalism, linguism, parochialism, and casteism are all raising their ugly heads, and the masses seem as far away from the classes as never before. Feudal ideas and attitudes still clog the land, and independent India appears to be developing into a peg on which we only hang our hats of personal ambitions. Surely, the salt cannot have lost its savour, India cannot have become false to its true values and the rat race cannot be the motive force of our development. Is it that we have failed somewhere in our planning? It is to this question that I propose to address myself in this chapter.

Economic growth is not just the result of financial outlays or of physical investments. It is the human being who has to utilize and operate the facilities created by investment, and it is the measure or ratio of response both to developmental needs and developmental operations that will determine the rate of economic growth. The one thing that has always struck me as a developmental economist, is the importance of the human factor in economic development. While capital and technology are both essential for growth, an equally important element is the way the human factor is harnessed for the purpose. Unlike other resources, human resources are almost infinitely elastic. Literacy, education, skills, as also health and nutrition, all undoubtedly add to the efficacy of the human factor. But the human being is more than a mixture of mind and matter. He has a soul, or if you prefer, a conscience. He has values. He dreams of a new and better world, and his dreams have a force and power that is more than that yielded by many millions of kilowatts of electric power of many thousands of tons of the most complicated machinery. This is what our sages in the past have called the "soul force." If only we can tap this force, release this idealism and sense of values, and harness it to our development programmes, we will get such a sense of fulfilment in our participation in the growth efforts that the whole development process will then become a grand and exciting adventure. The result will be, to use orthodox economic language, a drastic reduction in the disutility and real cost associated with work and saving. In other words, we can then get a far greater output in terms of goods and services and of individual and collective welfare, than we do now with our limited stock of natural and capital resources.

How do we release this non-material force that can make so much difference to our development effort? I suggest that we cannot do this unless we recognize that development is essentially a psychological phenomenon and that it is possible to build up this psychology even as one can construct a building or put up a factory or erect a dam or bring into existence a new university. Tawney has told us how Protestantism paved the way for the massive economic growth of the western world in his classic work on "Religion and the rise of Capitalism." We all know how the overthrow of feudalism and the attitudes and relations associated with it, restored to the human being, his sense of innate dignity and furnished the motive force for the vast strides that individual initiative and enterprise have made, not only in economic but also in social and scientific development. We are also aware how the early capitalist, unlovely as he sometimes was, nevertheless constituted a progressive force for economic growth by his sense of identification with his work and the subordination of his individual self to the larger purpose of building up his unit of business enterprise.

In more recent times, we have seen how a spirit of dedication to what was considered to be the larger social cause on the part of the ruling party, has transformed a socially and economically backward society into a modern, developed, and basically progressive nation, within the course of a little more than one generation. In every case the secret of success has lain in the free and purposive subordination of the individual to something higher and larger than himself, the institutionalization of personal ambition or the socialization of individual talent and incentives. The larger the number of people involved, the smaller the volume of current resources, and the more recent is the attempt at planned development, the greater becomes the necessity for this sublimation, and the release and nature of the psychological force for development. It is essential for a country going in for planned development to understand and realize the implications of the psychological basis for accelerated growth.

From the psychological point of view, there are three major factors that influence the volume and pace of economic growth, namely, willingness to put in the maximum amount of conscientious work, willingness to take risks and show enterprise in seeking opportunities for productive economic activity, and willingness to refrain from consuming more than a given proportion of the increase in income that accrues from economic development. The sectors involved are, broadly speaking, agriculture, industry, public administration, and the professions. The groups involved are, again in broad terms, owners of property, persons with enterprise, managers and administrators, and workers with varying degrees of skills. These could again be reclassified as the classes and the masses, the latter being much larger in number but disadvantaged individually in terms of income, levels of living, economic power and opportunity, and productive skills. Material planning creates opportunities for economic growth; it is the psychological response of the human factor that determines the utilization of these opportunities and therefore the volume and pace of economic growth.

Once we realize this basic fact, it becomes clear that the attitudes and behaviour of the human being constitute an important factor to which the planner must pay attention. Incentives is the generic expression which is used to indicate the factor that determines the response ratio of the human being to the opportunities created for economic development. Unfortunately incentives have become identified with money and individual advancement in material terms. Equally unfortunately, the scope of these incentives is largely confined to the leading sectors in economic growth of the middle and the upper classes, and the form it takes is one of individual material advancement. No one quite seems to realize that incentives for the classes may, by themselves prove to be disincentives for the masses, and that what we need is a complex of incentives that will motivate both the classes and the masses to play their proper role in speeding up the tempo of economic development.

In a country like India where the masses constitute the vast majority of the population and provide the bulk of its labour force and earners, there can be no massive development without their active and positive participation in the process of economic growth. Speeches and exhortations apart, our economic planning leans heavily on dynamizing the classes, leaving to the masses the role of hewers of wood and drawers of water rather than active and purposive participants. In a smaller country and with a smaller mass base of sub-standard levels of living dragging the economy, there is a lot to be said for the normal economic incentive of individual profits and incomes that can promote growth with stability not only because of the ladder from the bottom to the top that it establishes but also because of the reduction in the number and spacing of its rungs and the large numbers of the people who climb it.

There are only three countries in the world comparable to India in the size of their population. One of them has successfully adopted the capitalist way, but with an early start, a long period of gestation, and abundant natural resources. The other two, which started much later and with a heavy drag of mass povetry, have adopted the communist way, one with success and the other still to achieve it. The capitalist giant has used private property, freedom of enterprise and profit-seeking entrepreneurs and managers to build up its economy. The communist giants are using socialization of property, economic planning, and a large disciplined and dedicated party to build up their economies.

We in India function under a political democracy; we employ economic planning, and we use both the public and the private sectors to build up our economy. The incentives we use are appropriate to a capitalist economy but they have to function within the context of planning and its controls and a pronounced bias for the public sector. At the same time, we have not succeeded in drawing the masses into playing a positive role in the growth process. No doubt the classes are growing in strength and in numbers and our masses are recording some improvement in their levels of living, but the economic and social ladder is long, the rungs are many and their spacing is wide, and the frightful and frightening drag of mass poverty still clogs our economy.

To a social scientist like myself, who has always believed that India means its masses, the prospects of economic growth with stability and development with freedom seem more difficult today than before, unless we re-examine the psychological foundations of our economic planning, realize the integral place of social policy and development in economic growth, and rearrange our armoury of incentives and values in such a manner as will release mass energy, stimulate mass participation, and motivate mass involvement in the development process.

First and foremost, we have to restore to the individual among the masses a sense of human dignity and social equality. It is true we have given him political equality and this is proving to be an instrument for stimulating his desire for dignity and self-respect as also for social and economic equality. But unless social policies and institutions give him the opportunity for fulfilling these desires, we are only building up a mass force that will prove explosive one day and threaten our dream of development with freedom. Untouchability has been abolished by our Constitution, and we are making special budgetary provisions for the welfare and development of our Scheduled Castes and Scheduled Tribes.

But can we say with honesty that our caste Hindu society has succeeded in giving them a real sense of equality? Worse still, is there an active public opinion worrying itself about this problem and going all out to speed up the process of social equality and social development, especially in rural India? Passing laws and spending money by Government are both useful no doubt; but even more important is the change that we display in our hearts, our attitudes and our behaviour in daily life. Can we say that the spirit of Gandhiji permeates our relations with the people whom he called the *harijans*? These questions have only to be asked to give their answers. How can we make massive progress unless we give a stake and a sense of belonging to the 100 million people who constitutes our Scheduled Castes and Scheduled Tribes? It is true that this involves more than action by Government. But Government machinery can do a lot if its personnel, not only the bureaucratic but also the political, is permeated by the spirit of our Constitution in regard to the backward classes. Our students especially, can also make their contribution if only they can give the lead, by their conviction and behaviour, that untouchability and all that it stands for is a heinous social crime that has no place, not only in law but also in fact, in the new India that is theirs to build. It is not only the untouchable to whom we have not given a sense of human dignity and social equality. The whole caste system is an anachronism that is a standing slur on our attempts at achieving social equality and promoting social development. In addition, the country is cluttered with many feudal relics and attitudes that have no place in a democratic, let alone a socialist society.

An even greater cause of worry than the traditional princes, zamindars etc. is the new class of feudal princes—the political barons and bosses who live more than princely lives, demand and are given honours and homage traditionally given to the old feudal dignitories, and build a barrier between themselves and the common masses whom they propose to serve and in whose name they ascend to political power. What are we doing to build up a system of values that are rooted in dignity and individual human worth? Showpieces and special concessions are not the answer. What is needed is introspection and self-examination on our part and following it, a wholesale change in our entire attitude to the weaker and less privileged sections of our people as well as in our own way of living and behaviour.

Another imperative need is land reforms and giving the masses of our tillers rights of ownership which will involve them in a total way in the maximization of agricultural output. Nowhere in the world do we have such a large number of landless agricultural labourers, sharecroppers, and tenants as we have in India. "Land to the tiller" is a principle that has been implemented even in a land-starved and capitalist country like Japan. We have not yet succeeded in implementing this principle, though it has been accepted by Government and forms a basic component of our land policy. We have been talking of co-operative farming as a way of building up self-reliance, facilitating mobilization of resources and economic holding in agriculture and forging a link between land and the large number of tillers who either do not own it or do so in tragically small holdings. But we cannot claim so far even to have scratched the surface of co-operative farming in the country. All this may sound theoretical and possibly idealistic, but its psychological impact on production is unquestionable and therefore needs as much attention as the creation of material inputs if we want to involve the masses in our development programmes.

Adult literacy, especially in our rural areas, is another important prerequisite for development. According to the 1961 data, 71 per cent of males and 91 per cent of females in the rural areas are illiterate. Even the first estimates of the 1971 census do not place the overall literacy figures at more than 30 per cent. How can we expect them to have either the cultural or the social development that will release their inherent talent for the promotion of economic development? Literacy alone is not enough. We want functional literacy in the rural areas and this in turn requires a vast programme of book production in the regional languages and a reorientation of the entire educational system for serving the needs of the countryside.

In the absence of all this, what we are finding is not the growth of self-reliance and mass involvement in development, but the emergence of an agitational approach to economic problems and the building up of an unhealthy, and increasing reliance on government and governmental aid. Socialism does not mean statism, certainly not in the context of a democratic and free society. Unless our plans and policies result in self-reliance and self-help on the part of our masses, such development as we achieve by State initiative, government machinery and participation by the elite and the better off among our people, will not succeed in either solving the problem of mass poverty or creating a feeling of mass participation and mass involvement in the development process. It is time we re-examined our economic policies and programmes from this angle and gave more attention to the social and human aspects of our development planning.

Another hurdle in the way of development is the way we are building the elite class on the basis of monetary rewards and personal advancement and not on the basis of service or sublimation of personal ambition. Not that monetary in-

centives do not have an impact on the psychological forces
for greater effort. The only caveat is, that placed as we are
with our vast mass base of poverty, these incentives are only
resulting in widening the cleavage between the masses and
the classes, the town and the country, the backward and
the advanced regions, the elite and the others.

All this is helping to dilute the satisfaction that should
otherwise accompany the undoubted economic progress we
are achieving in aggregate terms, weakening the forces of
national unity and emotional integration, and leading to the
growth of a class consciousness that will soon make nonsense
of our efforts at building up a socialist society by consent
and evolution. Once we have established self-respect, human
dignity, social equality and self-reliance among the masses
of our people, especially those who live in our villages, broken
the back of our mass poverty and set up an effective economic ladder, then it would be time for monetary incentives
to be given a major play in stimulating the dynamism of those
who have the gifts for innovating, diversifying, and expanding our production apparatus.

Till then, the incentives we use for these economic builders
have to be different. Their satisfaction will have to come
largely from their identification with mass uplift, their sense
of social values, their feeling of pride and fulfilment in developmental effort, and their patriotism and love for India.
When we fought our battle for freedom, we did not think
in terms of material rewards, and the elite of the land poured
out in their thousands to mingle with the masses and set up
the great national ferment that ultimately brought us freedom. When the Chinese invaded our territory in October
1962, the whole nation rose and became one in thought and
feeling, the most advantaged among us were willing to merge
all that they had with the disinherited in the land.

Now we have to fight the battle against mass poverty and bring back dignity, self-respect, and social equality to the vast masses of our countrymen who have been for all too long, groaning under the shackles of feudalism, casteism, superstitions and other deterrents to human growth. Can we muster the courage and discipline that is needed to fight and win this battle? The country is still waiting for the answer.

It is strange that we have in India so little of voluntary or missionary effort on the part of those of us who are educated, better placed, or otherwise privileged. Long ago, the late Gopal Krishna Gokhale started a Servants of India Society. Today it languishes for want of fresh membership. Then again, the late Lala Lajpat Rai founded the Servants of People Society. We celebrate his centenary, but our offerings are in cash and institutions, not in men who will regenerate and expand the work that he started for educational uplift and social equality. Gandhiji founded many institutions and his followers have established the *Sarva Seva Sangh*, but one does not hear of a rush of recruits to these institutions or of the work they are doing for social development or social justice or the restoration of values. In our own days Vinobhaji started a class of *Jeevandanis*, but the movement has not caught on either in numbers or even in influence. In Bengal, a gifted son of blessed memory, Swami Vivekananda created the Sri Ramakrishna Mission for combining spirituality with service, and his missionaries have spread all over the land. But alas, their number is all too few, and there is difficulty in obtaining fresh recruits.

What has happened to us, the elite in India, that in spite of our boasted heritage of sacrifice, austerity and spirituality, there are so few that are found daring and disciplined enough to respond to the incentive of service and self-fulfilment in the sublimation of our personal ambitions and material de-

sires? Those amongest us who belong to the older age-groups
have a lot to answer for this state of affairs. Instead of re-
grouping for battle and reinforcing the social urges and idealistic fervour that gave us independence, we got bogged in
statecraft, politics, planning and undue reliance on governmental institutions and machinery. We forgot the crucial
role of the people, of values, of social and national urges, and
of idealism and voluntary action that alone can lead us to
the next victory of building up the society for which political
independence was but a prelude.

Someone said the other day that we are undergoing a crisis
of confidence. It would be more accurate to say that we are
going through a crisis in values. Must economic development
mean motivation of the classes only through economic incentives? If it does, we will not have either economic development on the scale we want, nor will it have that flavour that
comes from its contribution to the implementing of human
values. I refuse to believe however that the fountains of
idealism have dried up in the country or that only monetary
rewards can move the elite and the gifted among our people.
In a vast and poor country like ours, the elite have a much
greater public role than elsewhere, and their lives need to be
dictated much less by personal or private considerations.
Above all, they should think about what India means, what
India should mean, and what their own personal role is in
effecting the transition. India means her masses and patriotism means their service. What was said in the *Bhagwad
Gita* so many thousands of years ago holds true today with
even greater force:

यद्यदाचरति श्रेष्ठस्तत्तदेवेतरो जन: ।
स यत्प्रमाणं कुरुते लोकस्तदनुवर्तते ॥

(For whatsoever a great man does, that very thing other
men also do; whatever standard he sets up, the generality

of man follow the same).

It is therefore for the elite and the better placed as also the young of all classes to bind themselves to the service of the masses not merely by the functional use of their skills but also by their way of life, the sublimation of their personal ambition, their concern for social equality, and their willingness to be motivated by non-monetary incentives and accept a voluntary ceiling on their incomes.

How do we get our young people to adopt this new psychology for action? As has been mentioned earlier, sermons and exhortations do not provide the answer. Action programmes have to be devised for the deliberate stimulation of this psychology and that needs research of a far more extensive and productive character in personal and social dynamics than has been attempted so far by our social scientists. The only thing that is clear is that the human being is more than a mere economic man, that wealth and power are not the only mainsprings of human activity, and that there have been other motivations for hard work and sustained action that are traceable in both personal and social human history. It is values that constitute the missing link in our economic development and what is needed is the building of the psychological foundations which, stimulating material progress, also reconcile it with humanism and the best in the human heritage.

CHAPTER XIII

INDIA AND THE CHALLENGE OF DEMOCRATIC DEVELOPMENT

India is now setting out on the path towards becoming a modern, scientific, and industrial society. She has set before herself the task of doubling her national income in less than twenty years and her per capita income in less than twenty-five years. She has also placed before herself the task of building up during this period, a self-reliant, self-sustaining, and self-accelerating economy that will automatically ensure a satisfactory rate of annual economic growth without having to depend on foreign aid. She has taken to economic planning for the achievement of these objectives and has by now completed three Five Years Plans. She is currently engaged in operating a Fourth Five Year Plan.

Some of the major problems that India is facing in her attempt at rapid economic growth are the result of her determination to do this within the framework of democracy, which really means a "free society." The concept of freedom used in this context is quite comprehensive and has led me to give in another place, the following definition of a "free society":[1]

[1] "Freedom and Development—The Challenge," Australian Institute of International Affairs, 1960.

When we talk of a "free society," we mean a society where the common man is able to function with freedom in the most important and pervasive aspects of his daily life. This involves the possession by him of two fundamental freedoms. One is the freedom to determine the conditions of his work, protect his existing standard of living against any involuntary reduction, and also obtain for himself his due share in the increment of output resulting from increased economic activity. The other is the freedom to have that type of government which he can influence, if not actually control. Both these fundamental freedoms may be generically combined under the single phrase of 'democratic freedom', and require for their effective utilization such tool freedoms as an elected government, an independent judiciary, the rule of law, adult suffrage, freedom of association, including the right to form unions and resort to strikes, freedom of speech, freedom of press, freedom of movement and freedom of occupation.

Freedom in this sense is a comparatively new concept and did not exist in the early days of economic development. As we have repeatedly pointed out earlier in this volume, no major country, either capitalist or communist, has had a "free society" in this sense when it was going through its early and crucial stages of the transition from a pre-industrial to an industrial society. This is amply illustrated by the economic history of the United Kingdom, the United States, Germany, France, Japan, and the Soviet Union. Currently, China is providing a painful illustration of the same historical process. The transition from a pre-industrial to an industrial society in the economic sense, takes place earlier than the transition to a free society in the political sense. Everywhere, a free society seems to be an end-product of economic

growth. But we in India have perhaps been too ambitious—
I think however quite rightly—to go against the lessons of
economic history and set about attempting an acceleration
in our economic growth within the context of a "free society"
in the comprehensive sense in which I have used this phrase
earlier.

Thus the important thing to notice about India's attempt
at economic development is the political setting under which
it is taking place. From the adoption by India of her new
Constitution in November 1949, India has become a full-
fledged and operating democracy in the West European
sense of the term. India now has got adult franchise, and
has already had five general elections. In the fifth general
elections, which were held early this year, and for the first
time de-linked elections to State Assemblies from elections
to Parliament, the number of people voting was more than
151 million. It is evident from this figure that vast numbers
of industrial workers, poor peasants, and agricultural labourers are now in a position to influence government policy,
because they constituted the vast majority both of the electorate and of those actually voting.

Moreover, industrial labour occupies a peculiarly strong
position in the Indian polity. The number of members of
registered trade unions in India is as many as 2½ million
(contrast this with the fact that as late as 1930 there were
only 3 million trade union members in the United States)
and their political influence is considerable, not only because
of their organized strength but also because of the prominent
part they had taken in the fight for Independence, many of
them as members of the Congress Party. They now have a
footing in both the Federal and the State governments.

Consequently, we have in India, some of the most advanced labour legislation in the world. Various kinds of welfare

benefits are provided, including health insurance, provident fund, and facilities for recreation, while industrial housing is subsidized. Provision is made for both conciliation and adjudication of disputes and there are labour tribunals which can and do, in fact, order payment of bonuses to industrial workers from the profits that remain after meeting a prescribed return on capital invested in the concern. Thus, the industrial worker in India enjoys freedom and conditions of work and comparative wages at the initial stage of economic development such as his brother-workers in other countries did not enjoy at a similar period in their economic history.

A major problem resulting from this attempt at rapid economic growth within the context of freedom is the difficulty of increasing the domestic rate of saving to the required levels. The Planning Commission had set before the country the task of doubling the per capita national income in 23 years, a modest enough objective when it is remembered that the per capita income level from which planning started was less than 55 dollars. To achieve this objective they required the rate of investment to rise from about 6 per cent in 1950-1951 to 7.3 per cent in 1955-1956, 10.7 per cent in 1960-1961, 13.7 per cent in 1965-1966, 16.0 per cent in 1970-1971 and 17.0 per cent in 1975-1976.

Even if we assume a continuance throughout this period of substantial foreign aid, and expect it to remain as high as say 2 per cent of the national income by 1973-1974, this means a doubling of the rate of domestic saving in 23 years. Actually the rate of saving has to increase to a larger extent, partly because population is growing faster than anticipated by the Planning Commission and partly because the marginal capital-output ratios underlying the Planning Commission's income projections appear to be somewhat of an underestimate. Such a big increase in the rate of saving will not emerge voluntarily and will, therefore, require a substantial increase in taxation.

Moreover, it cannot be achieved without a substantial contribution from the less well-off sections of the community. Increasing the rate of taxation on the masses presents political difficulties because India has a parliamentary political democracy that functions actively. Getting a higher rate of savings from the masses also presents economic difficulties because their levels of current consumption are low, and their marginal propensity to consume is very high. Increasing the rate of taxation on the well-to-do and the rich also presents difficulties, because of its possible dis-incentive effects on the productive activities of the industrial elite, including not only the entrepreneurial but also the managerial, technological and bureaucratic classes. Getting a higher rate of personal saving from them is also difficult because of the demonstration effect of the ways of life of the economically developed western countries on these classes, and the identification in their minds of social prestige and status with display and conspicuous consumption.

This is the reason why the rate of domestic saving in India has not shown the kind of buoyancy that was expected of it. While no doubt, better organization of the savings and taxation machinery will have some effect, it is also clear that a profound change in the people's psychology is required to effect the required rise in the rate of savings and taxation in the country. The problems of education and institutional reorganization that this involves are immense and have not yet been tackled on the scale that is required.

Another problem that confronts India is the change that is required in mass attitudes to income and work. It would be correct to say that in one respect, the necessary change has been brought about in recent years. Thus, people are no longer content to accept poverty as their lot. Not only in urban but also in rural areas, there is great dissatisfaction on the part of the masses with their current economic status, and everywhere there is a perceptible rise in the demand for a better level of living.[2] The improvement that has taken place in the national average of consumption in the last ten years, even if marginal in content, has certainly added to this tendency. Along with this, there is a growing feeling of impatience with some of the customs or taboos that come in the way of increasing production, and a certain measure of readiness to try out new ideas and techniques. But in several other respects the position is not so satisfactory from the point of view of promoting economic growth.

Thus, recognition of the functional relationship between input and output is an essential condition for rapid economic growth. It means the cultivation of self-reliance, the feeling that it is one's own effort that determines the size of one's income. For this, it is necessary that the institutional structure of society is such as to discourage *rentier* incomes and give the worker the feeling that he is getting his due return for his work. Hence the important place that is assigned to land reforms (land to the tiller) in any programme of economic development. It is also necessary that persons who increase their inputs should have the confidence that their outputs will also increase and they will be getting their due share of the increased output, otherwise they will not be interested in increasing inputs and therefore in fostering economic growth.

Finally, it is necessary for the feeling to grow that income

---

[2] It is the perception of this fact that led the Indira Congress to coin the slogan "Quit Poverty" and made the abolition of mass poverty the central theme of its election manifesto in the 1971 elections.

cannot be increased merely by agitation or by gifts or by expropriation, and that, while equity should govern income distribution and may require agitation to get this done, it is even more important to increase output, not so much in national or group terms, but in individual and personal terms.

From this point of view, India is facing difficulties. There is still a widespread feeling that income is something which one is entitled to or gets as a favour rather than as something which is closely related to the input that one makes of labour, capital, enterprise, risk-taking, or any other economic factor. The long existence of foreign rule that discouraged individual initiative and gave no security of income, the popular religions that made man more a suplicant than a conqueror of nature and environment, the tradition that Marx refers to, of reliance on Government for public works, and the *ma-baap* legend encouraged by the British during their rule—all these make the Indian look up to Government rather than himself for his economic betterment.

This tendency has been reinforced by recent Indian political history, due to the emphasis placed by Indian leaders agitating against British rule, on governmental responsibility for Indian poverty, and the extravagant promises of governmental aid made by leaders seeking votes in quest of power under our democratic political set-up after independence. This tendency towards an agitational rather than an input approach to increase income, combined with a certain lack of economic self-reliance, constitutes one of the problems confronting the country in its transition from a pre-industrial to an industrial society. The problem is accentuated by the slowness of both the pace of land reforms in the country and of the movement towards co-operative production and worker participation in management. The presence of conspicuously visible incomes that do not seem to be the result of an adequate contribution on the part of their recipients is also adding to the difficulty.

In theory, the adoption of the goal of a socialistic society should have provided the necessary corrective; but in actual fact, a socialist society is still very far away. It is still the enunciation of an idea without spelling out its implications on individual conduct and way of life, and it has resulted merely in an agitation for better distribution rather than rallying the masses round the slogan of economic development and releasing their productive energies for the purpose.

A third difficulty confronting India is the rapid rate at which her population is growing. In the history of economic development, population growth was a normal feature and in fact made a positive contribution to economic growth. In the case of India, the position is somewhat different. Our numbers are already very large, and our long and continuous history has not left us with large reserves of unexploited land resources. Even a half per cent rate of growth in population would give India nearly 20 million more people in ten years. In actual fact, the recent census decade 1961-1971 has seen our population increase by nearly 108 million. The input of work and investment required to bring about an improvement in the economic condition of the existing population is itself very large because of the sheer size of the numbers involved and the very low absolute level from which we are starting. When, in addition, we have to take into account the added requirements represented by an increase in the population every ten years, of more than the entire population either of France or Great Britain or Germany, the problem of economic development becomes truly stupendous. An effort therefore has to be made to slow down the growth of the population.

One favourable feature of the situation is that the country is seized of the gravity of its population problem and the threat it poses to the building up of an industrial society. There is general unanimity regarding the need for family planning. A unique illustration of this can be found in the action taken by a leader of the opposition party in the Punjab Legislative Assembly, which, on the publication of the 1961 census results, moved a resolution expressing concern and asking for information on what action Government was taking to make a reduction in the birth rate. Family planning has a high priority in economic planning in India and ample funds are being provided for giving facilities to the population at large to go in for birth control. The recent census has also apparently shown that this is having some effect.

All the same, it takes time for these measures to yield appreciable results and meanwhile our economic planning is being adversely affected by this "population explosion." Thus, for example, the increase in India's per capita income over the first nine years of economic planning, which had been estimated at 16.5 per cent on the basis of previous projections of population growth, had to be revised downwards and brought down to 10.6 per cent on the publication of the preliminary results of the 1961 census. No similar exercize has been attempted so far for 1971 but in the projection for 1981 given in the Fourth Plan document, while national income is expected to double itself from its base in 1968-1969, the increase in per capita income is expected to be only 53 per cent in spite of an estimated significant reduction in the birth rate during the period.

Another difficulty that India faces is the hold that certain traditional institutions and historical forces still have on the Indian mind, and which are operating against the application of rationality to our programmes of economic development.

These forces are briefly described as casteism, linguism, and communalism. Though many of the traditional habits, inhibitions, and ways of life associated with casteism have now largely disappeared or are on the way to doing so, the sentiment of kinship and special relationship existing between the members of each caste still seem to persist. In fact, they appear to be taking on a new lease of life, thanks to the introduction of adult franchise and the uninhibited manner in which our parliamentary democracy is encouraged to function.

This kind of irrational sentiment, cutting across economic criteria of productive efficiency, comes in the way of rational utilization of economic resources and opportunities, and it makes difficult the establishment of an effective ladder based on efficiency and the required use of economic incentives in getting the best out of the human factor. The same kind of irrationality results from linguism and regionalism, with demands being made for the orientation of investment patterns on criteria other than of maximizing production or securing the quickest rate of national economic growth. Communalism is another irrational force that finds its strength from both majority and minority communties, and makes for a certain measure of political instability that is not conducive to economic growth.

It is true that the leaders of the country, notably the Prime Minister, are constantly attacking these forces of casteism, linguism and communalism, and pointing out the threat they constitute to rapid economic growth, apart from their inherent inconsistency within a good society. But these forces are basic and have behind them traditional and historical strength. It will take time to overcome them and replace them by a sentiment of common nationality that will function not only in the political but also in the economic field.

It must also be recognized that there are social and economic inequalities that have been connected with caste and regional inequalities that are now getting linked with language, as the constituent States of the Indian union have now been almost wholly reorganized on a linguistic basis. The obvious solution is the building up of the emotional integration of the country, based not only on materialist considerations of economic growth and political security, but also on cultural and traditional forces that would favour such an integration. It is also necessary to bridge the gaps in levels of living and economic opportunities that now exist among castes, communities, and regions, if one is to strike at the roots of these irrational feelings. The Government of India and the Planning Commission are taking steps to deal with these inequalities, but there is inadequate appreciation of their action. The normal working of the parliamentary democratic system, especially in the context of a federal government with its federal and state legislatures, also works in the direction of this inadequacy in appreciation.

I have no doubt that India will be able to meet the difficulties created by these retarding factors, but it will take time. It needs a much more extensive and organized attempt at public education than has been undertaken so far. It also requires a greater degree of attention to the institutional and psychological roots of these sentiments and a programme of action to combat them. In any case, their existence does cause obstacles in the way of economic development, and tends to slow down the rate of growth and prevent the extensive emergence of the spirit of rationality and economic calculation without which it is difficult to establish an industrial society.

Because economic development is now a matter for deliberate action in India and requires the prime role to be played by Government, a number of stresses, strains, and contradictions appear which make it difficult to pursue the goal of economic growth with the single-minded determination, comparable to the determination that emerged when it was fighting for survival in an armed conflict. Thus the large volume of unemployment and underemployment currently existing in the country combined with the massive additions that the increase of population is making to the labour force seeking employment, makes it imperative that a popularly elected government should pay primary attention to the provision of employment in its development programmes. But employment on a modern basis for such huge numbers requires a large volume of investment per worker, which is beyond our existing capacity. If employment nevertheless has to be provided on a large enough scale, investment that can be made available per worker will be very low, which means, in turn, that methods of production followed will be traditional rather than modern. which, in turn, means that we will not be creating an industrial society.

But an industrial society has to be created if we are to have economic growth. Our investible resources cannot therefore all be used merely for creating employment. Investment has necessarily to take the form of machinery, power, and technical know-how and thus help to create a modern sector in the economy. This leads inevitably to the emergence of a dual sector economy, one, modern, progressive and highly productive, and the other, traditional, backward and with low productivity. The relations between these two sectors such as competition, coordination, income levels, rates of advance, etc., all begin to constitute problems that are likely to present more difficulties than the creation of industrial societies did in the history of economic growth.

Allowing competition full play, letting wages fall and creating a large wage-seeking proleteriat is one possible way of dealing with this problem. Socializing the entire economy, pooling together all the output, whether from the modern or the traditional sector, and providing compulsory employment for everybody and compulsory markets for all output, is another possible way of dealing with the problem. But India does not believe in either of these solutions. She prefers a compromise; her approach is eclectic rather than dogmatic. She would adopt the ideal of a socialist society, but would couple it with a mixed economy with an ample play for private enterprise. She would go in for modernized methods of production and build up the components of a highly industrialized society. Simultaneously she would aid the traditional system, help to expand it, and seek to protect it from the competition of modern industry. A mixed economy with a public sector on the one hand and a private sector on the other, this is the uneasy compromise that is being forced on India by the size of her population, the limitations of her resources, and the laudable but difficult determination to achieve economic growth within the framework of a free society.

India is also facing the problem of creating an industrial elite in a hurry, which means producing a class of persons who will be enterprising, cost-conscious, dedicated to productivity, scientific-minded, and at home among machinery and modern industrial gadgets and processes. Indian upper class tradition has been literary and scholastic. The Indian educated person does not like rolling up his sleeves and wallowing in machinery, and the Indian image of highest success has been professional and bureaucratic rather than in industry and in the creation of material output. All this has to change if we are to succeed in setting up an industrial society in India. I must add that an industrial elite has started emerging, with the change in the upper class outlook becoming conspicuously noticeable in the last ten years. More and more Indians are taking to technical and scientific education, and some of them are shedding their allergy for manual work and the use of their hands and limbs. More Indians are also turning to industrial enterprise, and finance is gradually giving way to industrial manufacture as a better and more interesting way of making money. It is true that the desire for quick profits is still there and cost-consciousness is growing rather slowly, but it is growing and with it also the conciousness of productivity. The ambitious young Indian is now cheerfully going in for a business career; and the civil services and professions no longer claim the cream of Indian talent. The only snag in the process is that the motivations which are bringing about this change are the orthodox motivations of high incomes and more money. Science is growing but not, as Acharya Vinobha Bhave would want, alongside spirituality. On the contrary, declining spirituality and increasing inequality seems to be the price that India has to pay for introducing modernity into her society. This is a price that we do not want to pay. It is a price that, if paid, can only be at our peril and at the cost of those elements in our traditional society that are of permanent value and partake of the order of our eternal verities. Prime Minister Nehru, more than whom no man in Indian history has worked towards a modern and industrial Indian society, said in his thoughtful Maulana Azad memorial lecture on "India today and tomorrow":

But what I am concerned with is not merely our material

progress, but the quality and depth of our people. Gaining power through industrial processes, will they lose themselves in the quest of individual wealth and soft living? That would be a tragedy for that would be a negation of what India has stood for in the past and, I think, in the present time also as exemplified by Gandhi. Power is necessary, but wisdom is essential. It is only power with wisdom that is good.

All of us now talk of and demand rights and privileges, but the teaching of the old *dharma* was about duties and obligations, rights only following duties discharged and not obtaining divorce from the latter.

Can we combine the progress of science and technology with this progress of the mind and spirit also? We cannot be untrue to science, because that represents the basic fact of life today. Still less can we be untrue to those essential principles for which India has stood in the past throughout the ages. Let us then pursue our path to industrial progress with all our strength and vigour and, at the same time, remember that material riches without toleration and compassion and wisdom may well turn to dust and ashes. Let us also remember that "Blessed are the Peace-Makers." And yet, we do not know what will be the ultimate system that will emerge in India when she has completed her transition from a backward to a developed society.

To sum up, the problems that confront India in her onward and deliberate advance towards economic development are truly more formidable than those which have encountered the growth or creation of any other developed society in the world. And it is the Indian challenge of development with democracy, progress with stability, and growth without violence, that is the most noteworthy characteristic of the contemporary Indian picture. How the challenge will end, I do not know. Perhaps Norman Brown has the answer, when basing himself on a study of Indian history, he says this of India:

> She can keep the old, if it is useful, because she can also uncomplainingly give up the old when it is no longer useful. She does not have to experience a violent conversion, get rid of all her past at once, and suddenly become something different. She can instead progress by successive steps, even by steps taken in quick succession, as at present. She can always be adapting herself, without experiencing a devastating feeling of guilt in doing so...or so, at least I surmise.

Recent events, with the simultaneous emergence of naxalism and the recent repudiation of left as well as right extremism by the electorate, leaves one with mixed feelings regarding the future. But I am rash enough to believe that Norman Brown will prove right and that India will succeed in bringing about the needed social and economic transformation without either repudiating the past or using violence to bring about the future, though I must also confess that my belief is based more on a mystic faith in the destiny of my country rather on a scientific and rational assessment of its current position and its future prospects.

APPENDIXES

PLEDGES TO THE PEOPLE

Extracts from the speech delivered by Jawaharlal Nehru in the Constituent Assembly, New Delhi, 14 August 1947, on the eve of the attainment of independence.

Long years ago we made a tryst with destiny, and now the time comes when we shall redeem our pledge, not wholly or in full measure, but very substantially. At the stroke of the midnight hour when the world sleeps, India will awake to life and freedom. A moment comes, which comes but rarely in history, when we step out from the old to the new, when an age ends, and when the soul of a nation, long suppressed, finds utterance. It is fitting that at this solemn moment, we take the pledge of dedication to the service of India and her people and to the still larger cause of humanity.

That future is not one of ease or resting but of incessant striving so that we may fulfil the pledges we have so often taken and the one we shall take today. The service of India means the service of the millions who suffer. It means the ending of poverty and ignorance and disease and inequality of opportunity. The ambition of the greatest man of our generation has been to wipe every tear from every eye. That may be beyond us, but as long as there are tears and suffering, so long our work will not be over.

THE CONSTITUTION OF INDIA

Extracts from the Directive Principles of State Policy.

Article

(38) The State shall strive to promote the welfare of the people by securing and protecting as effectively as it may, a social order in which justice, social, economic and political, shall inform all the institutions of the national life.

(39) The State shall, in particular, direct its policy towards securing:

(a) that the citizens, men and women equally, have the right to an adequate means of livelihood;

(b) that the ownership and control of the material resources of the community are so distributed as best to subserve the common good;

(c) that the operation of the economic system does not result in the concentration of wealth and means of production to the common detriment;

(d) that there is equal pay for equal work for both men and women;

(e) that the health and strength of workers, men and women, and the tender age of children are not abused and that citizens are not forced by economic necessity to enter avocations unsuited to their age or strength;

(f) that childhood and youth are protected against exploitation and against moral and material abandonment.

(40) The State shall take steps to organize village panchayats and endow them with such powers and authority as may be necessary to enable them to function as units of self-government.

(41) The State shall, within the limits of its economic capacity and development, make effective provision for securing the right to work, to education and to public assistance in cases of unemployment, old age, sickness and disablement, and in other cases of undeserved want.

(42) The State shall make provision for securing just and humane conditions of work and for maternity relief.

(43) The State shall endeavour to secure, by suitable legislation or economic organization or in any other way, to all workers, agricultural, industrial or otherwise, work, a living wage, conditions of work ensuring a decent standard of life and full enjoyment of leisure and social and cultural opportunities and, in particular, the State shall endeavour to promote cottage industries on individual or co-operative basis in rural areas.

(45) The State shall endeavour to provide, within a period ten years from the commencement of this Constitution, for free and compulsory education for all children until they complete the age of fourteen years.

(46) The State shall promote with special care the educational and economic interests of the weaker sections of the people, and, in particular, of the Scheduled Castes and the Scheduled Tribes, and shall protect them from social injustice and all forms of exploitation.

(47) The State shall regard the raising of the level of nutrition and the standard of living of its people and the improvement of public health as among its primary duties and, in particular, the State shall endeavour to bring about prohibition of the consumption, except for medicinal purposes, of intoxicating drinks and of drugs which are injurious to health.

(48) The State shall endeavour to organize agriculture and animal husbandry on modern and scientific lines and shall, in particular, take steps for preserving and improving the breeds, and prohibiting the slaughter of cows and calves and other milch and draught cattle.

EXTRACTS FROM THE INDIAN NATIONAL CONGRESS ELECTION MANIFESTO, 1971

The General Election of 1967 registered the people's impatience with the pace of progress in India. In spite of the many achievements that stood to the credit of the Congress and the people—vast and complex industrial enterprises, agrarian reforms, mass education including expansion of university and technical education, and major social reforms and advancements in many other spheres, particularly in science and technology—many vital and important problems remained to be tackled. Millions continued to live in poverty and backwardness. Justice—social, economic and political—which is the basis of our Constitution remained yet a goal to be fought for and attained. It was not surprising that all this was reflected in the polls of 1967.

After the General Election of 1967, important and far-reaching political developments took place because of the tremendous mass upsurge and awakening. Only a genuine radical programme of economic and social development could meet the challenge of this new situation. It is in this context that the Congress formulated the Ten-Point Programme and pledged itself to implement it effectively and speedily.

But these moves by the Congress to accelerate the pace of social and economic reforms aroused the opposition of vested interests and their advocates. Conservative elements inside the Congress organization, who were averse to and afraid of change, reacted sharply. When they became aware of our determination to implement the basic policies and radical programmes which had earlier been decided upon jointly, they left and combined with those who had most bitterly opposed all that the Indian National Congress had stood for and fought for under the leadership of Mahatma Gandhi.

The Congress is firmly convinced that the challenges posed by the present critical situation can be met only by the proper and effective implementation of a social and economic programme through democratic processes. The Congress wishes to emphasize that the policies and programmes to which it stands pledged are in accordance with the principles laid down in the Constitution of India.

The nation's progress cannot be halted. The spirit of democracy demands that the Constitution should enable the fulfilment of the needs and urges of the people. Our Constitution has earlier been amended in the interest of economic development. It will be our endeavour to seek such further constitutional remedies and amendments as are necessary to overcome the impediments in the path of social justice.

The Congress, therefore, appeals to the people to return its candidates to the Lok Sabha and thus give it a clear mandate to:

(i) continue the advance to socialism through democratic processes and devise an administrative system capable of speeding implementations;

(ii) put down the forces of violence and disorder so that all our citizens can live in peace and harmony;

(iii) defend secularism and safeguard the interests of the minorities and the weaker sections of the community, particularly the Scheduled Castes, Scheduled Tribes and the other backward sections so that they may attain "equality of status and opportunity and fraternity assuring the dignity of the individual";

(iv) end anachronistic privileges such as privy purses etc. and reduce glaring disparities of income and opportunity;

(v) accelerate efforts to provide basic requirements to our people by undertaking a dynamic programme of agricultural development by the application of science and technology and thereby usher in a new phase of rural prosperity, which will improve the condition of small farmers, farmers in dry areas, the landless, artisans and others who eke out their existence through diverse skills;

(vi) provide fresh avenues of employment and thus widen the participation of our citizens in nation-building activities;

(vii) enlarge the role of the public sector and improve its performance.

The Congress is the only party which can place its programme before the people with a sense of responsibility. The Congress pledges itself anew to these challenging tasks to a social revolution which is peaceful and democratic and embraces all our people and permeates all spheres of national life. The Congress is the only party which has the capacity to achieve such a social revolution.

The people have the power. They are now called upon to choose the programme and the party which can best serve their interests. We appeal to the pepole once again to give us their mandate.

Poverty must go. Disparity must diminish. Injustice must end. These are but essential steps towards our ultimate goal—the goal of an India which is united and strong, an India which lives up to its ancient and enduring ideals, yet is modern in thought and achievement, meeting the future with vision and confidence.

EXTRACTS FROM THE ADDRESS BY THE PRESIDENT OF INDIA TO PARLIAMENT, 23 MARCH 1971

The General Election has once again demonstrated that durable political power in a democracy has only one source—the people.

...Our people have made their choice.... And theirs is a massive mandate for change, peaceful change that must swiftly and visibly alter the picture of poverty and alienation in our land.

We have begun this work. But now we have to address ourselves afresh to evolving perspectives, policies and practices even more closely and concretely related to the needs of our people and our times.

My Government have been returned to office on the clear pledge that the central objective of our policy must be the abolition of poverty. To achieve this, my Government are firmly committed to implementing the economic and social transformation outlined in the manifesto which has received such overwhelming support of the electorate.

...To achieve victory in the war against poverty and social injustice requires the sustained and dedicated efforts of the millions of our people. I am confident that Members of Parliament and the people of India, as a whole, will respond, in abundant measure, to the challenge of our times.

INDEX